DIPS OF WATER FROM THE WELLS OF LIFE

104 Stories —
A Mixture of Humor and Holiness

by
Crate Jones

Produced by

JM Productions

ISBN 0-939298-35-X

Order additional copies from:
Crate Jones
3106 Appling Way
Durham, NC 27703

Cover drawing by Denny Frye, Raleigh, NC
Cover design by Joe Allen Designs, Nashville, TN

Unless otherwise indicated all scripture references are from *The King James Version* of the Holy Bible.

All references marked NIV are from *The Holy Bible, New International Version.* © Copyright 1973, 1978, 1984 by International Bible Society.

All references marked NKJV are from The Holy Bible, New King James Version. Copyright © 1982 by Thomas Nelson, Inc.

Reference to *Amplified New Testament* are from *The Amplified New Testament,* © 1958, The Lockman Foundation.

The reference marked NRSV is from The New Revised Standard Version of the Bible. Copyright © 1989 by the Division of Christian Education of the National Council of Churches.

Author's paraphrases are indicated as such.

With Thanksgiving to God,
This Book Is Dedicated To Our Seven
Grandchildren

Mark
Daniel
Valerie
Taylor
David
Christopher
Melanie Ann

Our Grand-Children

"For of such is the Kingdom of Heaven"
—Jesus

Harriett at 18

PREFACE

Dips of Water from the Wells of Life is a sequel to my other books, *Out of the Crate* and *Tall Truths from Short Stories*.

The book is a collection of short stories, written about true events — events that are personal experiences, experiences I have observed or heard. All of these have been woven into stories appealing to the mind and heart of the reader.

In desiring the book to set the truth of Scripture in real-life situations, selected verses are used throughout the book.

Some of the stories contain humor. Christianity is joyful, and humor is God-given. Laughter is needed for a healthy spirit. Each humorous story leads to a more serious thought.

Other stories are in a more serious vein. They deal with various emotions that touch the lives of many people. At times, nostalgia is aroused through a story that stirs a memory. All of the stories have an application to life.

I am indebted to my wife, Harriett, for encouragement, her many helpful suggestions, her contributions to the stories, and her prayer support. We have worked on the book together and want these stories to please the Lord and to be helpful to the reader.

Gratitude belongs to the many friends who have encouraged the writing of another book, to those who have endorsed the work, to Frances Wells for her patient proofreading, and to Joe Johnson, former editor with Broadman Press, for his valuable assistance, professional counsel, and conviction that the book should be published. Also to Denny Frye, North Carolina State Fair Woodcarver, for the artwork of the old well.

As the book goes on its journey, all thanksgiving belongs to our Heavenly Father from Whom all our blessings come.

May a bit of light from Heaven shine through these "windows" into your soul, and may Jesus Christ be praised.

I sought the guidance of the Holy Spirit in preparing this book. As you read it, He will enable you to "listen with your heart."

Jesus said, "The water that I shall give him shall be in him a well of water springing up into everlasting life."(John 4:14).

It is my prayer that, through the stories contained in this book, the reader will have a taste of that water and see Him who is the Giver of everlasting life.

—Crate Jones

FOREWORD

Shakespeare noted that there are "sermons in stones." He might have included almost everything if we are spiritually sensitive to see them. If you want proof of this, I challenge you to read this book. Crate Jones has that sensitivity. He has the rare gift of seeing the sacred in the commonplace. Once you start reading this volume you will not want to put it aside until you have read the final page.

Pastors will find it to be a *mother lode of sermon starters*. Also it is a storehouse of vivid illustrations. Illustrations make a sermon live. Truths derived from them are seldom forgotten. After 68 years in the preaching ministry, I have found this to be true. Jesus Himself presented some of His greatest and best-remembered truths by building them around parables dealing with everyday things that surround us.

What about those who are not preachers? This book will serve as reading matter in your daily devotions, but do not simply take my word for it. Try it for yourself and you will join me in thanking the author for blessing your life and for enabling you to see God's goodness and message in even the simplest things along the pathway of life.

— Herschel H. Hobbs
Oklahoma City, Oklahoma
Pastor; Author; Past President,
Southern Baptist Convention

ENDORSEMENTS FOR
Dips of Water from the Wells of Life

There are few current writers I enjoy more than Crate Jones for simple inspiration and refreshment. When one is tired or exceptionally busy, it is good to be able to pick up a book like Crate's which is not only easy to read but makes you feel as if you'd had a visit with a wonderful family.

—Ruth Bell Graham
Montreat, North Carolina

I was editor of inspirational/trade books for Broadman Press for almost 23 years, editing 590 different books and working with hundreds of authors.

I would hope by now that I have an insight into what constitutes excellent, well-crafted writing. Crate Jones is a master at writing to-the-point, timely illustrative stories, all of them based on reality. He has previously published *Out of the Crate* and *Tall Truths from Short Stories*. I had the privilege of serving as his editor on *Tall Truths*.

I honestly believe people are hungry for down-to-earth, humorous, and pungent material like his. His stories make superb resources for all types of speaking, preaching, and teaching. Above all, though, his stories are highly enlightening and entertaining for a wide cross-section of readership.

Without the slightest hesitation I unequivocally recommend *Dips of Water from the Wells of Life.*

—Joseph S. Johnson
Author-Editor-Editorial Consultant
Editor of Inspirational/Trade Books, Broadman Press
(Retired)

For the past thirty years it has been my privilege to know Crate Jones and to work with him in a variety of ways: fellow pastor; committee member; denominational service and personal friend. During these past months Crate has been Interim Pastor of the church where my wife and I are members. In every relationship Crate has brought good humor, keen insights, and a depth of spiritual maturity.

In his latest book, *Dips of Water from the Wells of Life*, Crate reveals his unusual gift of "seeing a sermon" in the ordinary experiences of life. Here one will encounter wit, humor, challenge, theology, wisdom and just plain common sense. Through it all Crate calls to attention the graciousness of God and His dealings with people of all ages in all kinds of circumstances.

I commend this latest from the pen of Crate Jones to pastors and laity alike. These insightful essays will prove a blessing to all who will read them.

—Roy J. Smith
Executive Director-Treasurer
Baptist State Convention of North Carolina

A. Purnell Bailey, D.D.
Syndicated Columnist

October 3, 2001

Dear Crate,

Your *Dips of Water from the Wells of Life* is a blessing to me. I keep it on my desk and dip from it again and again—to prime my pump!

In your 104 stories of "a Mixture of Humor and Holiness" you draw from some deep wells. Humor and wholeness is what the world could use these days.

Thank you again for sharing with me these words from your life and your pen.

Gratefully,

—Dr. A. Purnell Bailey
Methodist Minister
Retired Army Chaplain with First Cavalry Division
Author of <u>Daily Bread Devotions</u>
Writer of "Daily Bread" carried by many newspapers

CONTENTS

Section 5
On Being A Child **81**

Section 6
Floating Memories **107**

Section 7
Listen To Your Teachers **133**

Section 8
Church Happenings **153**

SECTION 1

Love: God's Superglue

Superglue

Six-and-a half-year-old grandson, Taylor, is an inexhaustible source of story ideas. Some of them are like little telescopes that bring heavenly truths into view.

Grandmama's privileges include being storyteller, playmate, and good friend to Taylor. Invisible golden cords of love secure the bond between them. This was expressed in a way never before heard, one of those "I'll-not-forget-that-one" times.

By way of birth, some of Grandmama's blood flows in his veins. That makes her a real part of him in a way that cannot be broken. What took place on a certain memorable day depended on that relationship.

Grandmama was getting ready to leave Taylor for a little while. He sidled up to her and said, "I wish I had some superglue." Practical Papa was on the verge of explaining how dangerous superglue can be. His words of wisdom died aborning. Wise and patient Grandmama asked, "What would you do with it?" He said, "I'd glue myself to you."

What an expression of love and wanting to be close to the one loved! Talk about togetherness.

Then the elevator of the Spirit carried the whole episode a few stories upward. A picture of Jesus and those who love Him and belong to Him began to develop.

Through our blessed experience of salvation, we are born again and become a beloved member of the family of God. According to Scripture, "Christ lives in us" (Galatians 2:20). The life of Jesus now flows in our spiritual veins. An unbreakable relationship with Him is established.

Seeing as how we are related to Jesus, in Him we are also kin to one another. We become one in the bond of love. I reckon that means I'd best be particular to treat all my kinfolks with kindness, just like Jesus does. It means whatever I do to one in whom the forgiving Savior lives, I am doing to Him. Jesus said so (Matthew 25:40).

With that Savior-believer relationship, we have the certainty of His Presence. The "superglue" is just one of His always-kept promises: "I am with you always" (Matthew 28:20). That means no matter what, He's there: good times, bad times; sunshine, shadows; health, sickness; loved or unloved; excluded by others or included. He's our Friend who sticks closer than a brother. It's a superglue relationship!

What tenderhearted little Taylor wished for externally, Jesus has done for us internally. We don't have to *wish* we were "glued" to our Savior. We *are*! Glory be! We'll never come unglued!

On Being Wanted

It was a parable in motion that lodged in my mind.

A motor home was on its merry way, carrying a vacationing family toward some destination. Following behind, securely attached by a towbar, was a Samurai Suzuki, sort of a fourth cousin to a Jeep. Emblazoned on the spare wheel cover were the words, "ME, TOO."

Several thoughts hooked up in my head. Little "Sam" was saying, "I belong to this outfit. I'm needed, I'm wanted, and I'm cared for. Whoopee!" A moving picture of being included.

Wanting to belong is ingrained in the human spirit. From the beginning, God said, "It is not good for man to be alone." Being rejected hurts like all get out. Any kid who's been ignored in games knows the feeling.

As a scrawny, undersized youngun, I was to learn a fella can have athlete's foot without having athletic feet. Ball games on the local commons usually left me on the sidelines or having the dubious honor of being chosen last. My "Me, too?" was met with "Are you kidding?" That puts a dwarfing on our self-esteem — stirs up that unwanted feeling.

The world is full of rejected people who wear a scarlet "R" in their hearts. One of the saddest verses in the Bible is this: "I looked on my right hand, and beheld, but there was no man that would know me: refuge failed me; no man cared for my soul" (Psalm 142:4).

Rejection is found among the elderly, the abandoned wife or husband, homeless children, street people, the jobless. Every little aborted baby's "Me, too" was stamped with an irrevocable "unwanted."

All of us have been unwanted at times, but there is One who had a penchant for seeking out the unloved to show them caring love. He still does. Who is He? His name is Jesus. Echoing down time's corridor are His words, "He that cometh to Me, I will in no wise cast out" (John 6:37). What welcome words to those who have felt unwanted, unwelcome, and unneeded.

When a boy of nine, I heard His invitation to give Him my heart. "Me, too, Lord?" "You, too, son," He replied. And He has never made me feel unwanted.

In Christ, we travel life's highway singing, "Me, too; Me, too!"

The Discarded Teddy Bear

'Twas a pitiful sight. A little teddy bear lying face down in the gutter, arms and legs pointing in four directions. He appeared to be rainsoaked.

While I was leading a funeral procession, the castaway teddy caught my eye briefly. Quickly some bare truths began to bear on my mind. My thoughts were on the reality of death, but then a parable of life began to intermingle. Life itself is an intermingling of the two.

Although I didn't know the story of the little fella's journey from the time of his creation to his being tossed into the gutter, several facts were self-evident.

He was meant to bring joy to a little child or even to an elderly person regressing to childhood. Teddy bears and cuddling go together like cubs and dens. They are soft, happy looking, and they stir chords of love. If they could "bearly" talk, "I need you to love me" would probably be heard. To this one, somebody had said, "I don't love you anymore."

Now, teddy bears were never intended to end up in a gutter, for they were meant for higher destinies.

Stopping the procession was impossible, but the urge to "rescue the perishing" tugged at my heartstrings. Slamming on the brakes might have caused a demolition derby and made folks wonder what had happened to my mind.

But I wanted to pick him up, clean him up, dry him off, and put him in a pair of little arms somewhere.

Then the parable took on flesh and bones. When God took some dust and made a man out of it (Genesis 2:7), the human race got off to a fine beginning. He equipped His new creation with an innate hankering to be loved.

Alas, the ol' serpent slithered into Eden's garden, and something went haywire. The pristine pair was duped into believing God hadn't been truthful. Believing Satan's lie, Adam and Eve let sin make a grandiose, though subtle, entrance into humanity's heart.

From the time Cain permanently disabled brother Abel, the "King of the Hill" types have treated other folks like things to use, abuse, and throw away. Just like the hapless little bear. Because of somebody's inhumane treatment, folks, created in the image of God, have been dehumanized and gutterized. Folks, little, old, and in-between.

For those who have been made to feel unloved and discarded, here is a promise to claim: "The Lord is close to the broken-hearted and saves those who are crushed in spirit" (Psalm 34:18, NIV).

Like the little discarded bear, there are hurting folks everywhere, needing a caring heart, a lifting hand, and someone to "tell them of Jesus, the mighty to save." He lifts us from the gutter to glory. Praises be!

Jesus: Treasure Hunter

Adventure. The word stirs the imagination and quickens the pulse. Spawns visions of danger, risk, fulfilled dreams.

Such was the content of a TV newscast. The reporter (Carole Simpson) whetted the curiosity of the viewers with interest-catching teasers before commercial breaks. "From down in the depths, coming up rich." "A sparkling recovery from a stormy past."

The commercials vanished, the story she told remains. A Spanish galleon had sunk 258 years ago off the Florida Keys. Much treasure had long since been salvaged, but one treasure-hunting diver believed there was more.

Patiently, painstakingly, he searched, finding numerous religious artifacts, jeweled rosaries, gold rings crafted for nuns, and other precious articles. His retrieval is worth millions of dollars.

One special note of interest revealed the hunter's attention to minute detail. From a beautiful, jewel-adorned necklace, the cross was missing. "A piece small enough to be swallowed by a fish," said the commentator. Believing it was down there, the tenacious diver said, "We'll find it." Seeing the pictures of his ocean-floor probing, he probably did.

What a beautiful analogy of the Lord Jesus and His unceasing search for lost humanity. In His sight, we are lost treasure. In coming to earth, He followed a trail which led to the cross. There, He "pain-takingly" bore our sins in His own body. "By whose stripes we are healed" (1 Peter 2:24).

Jesus is the tireless "Hunter" who goes to the deep, dark places of the earth, searching for precious souls, buried in sin. It's His reason for coming to this world. It can be said of the one having been found, who responded to His loving reach, "From down in the depths, coming up rich!"

Rich in two ways. The salvaged life is rich beyond measure, and Jesus claims us as His jewels. Malachi puts it this way: "They shall be mine in that day when I make up my jewels" (3:17).

Again, many a life has been shipwrecked, lying in comparative ruins for years. Some raging storm made havoc of what that life could have been. But Jesus says, "I will search until I find even that one missing piece." (In the Book of Luke, Jesus tells of the search for one lost sheep, one lost coin, one lost boy, and of the jubilation upon finding them.)

When the mission is accomplished, there follows the triumphant shout, "A sparkling recovery from a stormy past!" For a sin-encrusted life becomes a sparkling jewel in the Master's hand.

This eternal treasure's estimated value? Priceless!

God's Love and an Umbrella

Epistle writer James writes about hooking faith and works in tandem so faith becomes visible. Says he, "If a brother or sister be naked, and destitute of daily food, and one of you say unto them, 'Depart in peace, be ye warmed and filled; not withstanding ye give them not those things which are needful to the body; what doth it profit?" (2:15-16).

The answer is "not much." He says faith without works is dead. The same goes for love.

The idea is the needy person won't be much taken with religious talk unless it's backed up with garb and grub.

It happened between Asheboro and Seagrove, North Carolina, on a rainy day. He was hoping for a ride. His earthly possessions were tied up in a couple of bedrolls. The urge to pick him up hit, so he was invited to get in.

We had about ten miles together before our destinations reached a different direction. His story was heart-touching: homeless, jobless, divorced, sleeping in shelters and under bridges, and now on the way to Florida. He figured at least he wouldn't freeze there.

His "No" answer to my question, "Do you know Jesus as your Savior?" opened a door of opportunity to tell him of God's love and the death of Jesus for our sins.

The usual parade of reasons (?) was expressed. "It's not for me," he said. There was some hope for "death-bed repentance," but who has the assurance of such a chance? His response that to receive Christ would give him a new and better life was, "I'll leave it like it is." He made his choice in spite of the obvious difference Jesus would make. I assured him that God did not want him to waste his life as he was doing.

My guest was polite, asking for nothing. He had had a couple of packs of Nabs that day and refused the offer of stopping for a sandwich.

"Do you have any money?" Smiling, he said, "I have about five rusty pennies, which I probably couldn't spend."

James' conscience-pricking words stirred around in my mind and God's love moved in my heart. I gave him some money, which he took reluctantly. Then I heard the Spirit saying, "And give him your umbrella." Again there was a look of wonder on his face, but he accepted the gift.

We parted. I waved to him as he stood by the road's edge, and I saw him no more.

What a contrast. Because of Jesus, I have found purpose in life, my needs are taken care of, and heaven is my destination. Without Jesus, the man who briefly crossed my path is without these essentials. Jesus could change all of that.

As I traveled on, tears filled my eyes, and I prayed, "Oh God, help me lead people to Jesus." I felt a sense of failure.

I wonder where my friend is now? My hope is that the words shared somehow found a fertile spot in his heart. The money couldn't have lasted very long, but maybe each time he looks at the umbrella or stands beneath its shelter, he will remember the final words, "God loves you." And maybe one day he will say, "He does? Why, yes, He does!"

That's my prayer.

For You, Anytime!

Christopher, two, and David, five, were acting like normal brothers. The older one was throwing small goldfish crackers at the little one. Daddy Russell rebuked the thrower, telling him to stop.

David then tried to just hand his brother another cracker, and it fell on the floor. All Daddy saw was the little edible fish hit the floor. Assuming disobedience had taken over, he got after him again.

Knowing he was innocent of the charge, David sidled up to Mama Lori and said, "I'm upset with Daddy." From his little wounded heart, truth poured out. He hadn't done what he was accused of doing. Daddy was informed of the mistake.

Here's where the wheels of confession and forgiveness were set in motion. An injustice had taken place. Russell's heart pained him; things had to be made right.

He said, "David, I was wrong; I'm sorry. Will you forgive me?" The little fella responded in a classic way. Cocking his forefinger and thumb and pointing them good-naturedly at his repentant Dad, he said, "For you, anytime."

What a legacy. A father big enough to admit it when he was wrong and humble enough to ask forgiveness of a little child. David will grow up with that indelible lesson tucked away in his heart. The air was cleared, fellowship was restored, and the whole matter was put away. There was joy in the household, and love flowed like a refreshing stream.

Ultimate forgiveness is seen at that heart-wrenching scene of Calvary and the cross. Jesus was dying, pouring out His blood in payment for our sins. Two condemned men, one on either side of that central cross, were paying for theirs. One felt the tug of conviction and cried, "Lord, remember me when You come into Your kingdom!"

With a nail-impaled hand pointing in the direction of the repentant, the suffering Savior replied, "Today you will be with Me in paradise!" Was He not saying, "For you, anytime!"

To visualize the cross, with Jesus the Great Forgiver thereon, should cause our hearts to be more tender toward our fellow travelers. Many a broken friendship would be restored, if all of us offenders would admit our need for forgiveness from God and man. Self-righteous, looking-down-our-noses at stumbling pilgrims would melt in the warmth of God's love.

And the beauty of it all is that the door of forgiveness is open to all who have offended or been offended. When we say, "I'm sorry; will you forgive me?" the gracious Savior gladly says, "For you, anytime."

That, then, becomes the attitude of the heart toward others. Being forgiven, we forgive. A loving-hearted little boy has shown us how to react toward someone who needs our forgiveness. Refusing to do so causes the heart of the refuser to be locked up in the prison house of torment. Jesus is the key that unlocks the door "for you, anytime!"

SECTION 2

When Things Go Wrong

Smudges and Glitches

Hospital stays often prove that high-tech equipment is not always foolproof. It can be kind of April-foolery, making the puny person the butt of an unintentional joke.

For instance, the hunt was on for whatever might be out of whack in my insides. One chest X-ray ran up a red flag. "Spot on right lung." Uh oh! T.B. or not T.B.? That is the question. Or maybe another kind of intruder.

Since I am internally photogenic, close to ten or more spooky portraits were shot. The spot was nowhere to be found. Glory be! Could it be a miracle? Could be, but not this time. A bright sleuth solved the mystery: somebody's finger smudge. The old-time medicine man's magic potion couldn't effect a cure any faster than that. I was as relieved as some guy who swallowed a carton of Rolaids to know my "bellows" were unspotted.

Another for instance: those tape printouts from a cardiogram can be a mite unnerving. Mine looked like the thing had gone berserk. From normal scratches to stretches that resembled sure-nuff trouble, near 'bout running off the page. Looked like a lovesick teenager's heartbeat, or maybe like mine was about to blow its top, as did Mt. Vesuvius.

Truth to the rescue. It was a glitch in the machine. I wasn't as bad off as it appeared. Another test showed the ol' ticker was hittin' with band-like rhythm.

Now between smudges and glitches, I had been considerably discomfited. Both first reports were deduced from falsehood. And that on tax-due day to boot.

The doctor summed it up right well. "As long as there are computers, there will be a need for man. They will never take his place, for they came from man." He went on writing his notes, unaware that he had uttered a profundity.

The cogs in my cranium began to mesh. There's a connection between what had happened and what the doctor said that points to a heavenly truth. Namely: As long as there is man, there will always be a need for God. He will never take God's place, for he came from God.

Trying to live independently of God, man creates smudges and glitches for himself and others. His resulting actions are dictated by falsehood rather than truth. Not only is such a person's equipment crossed up, its not even plugged in.

Enter man's acknowledged need for God. For God knows how to fix His own created being's "inner computer" so smudges and glitches will be few, and truthful readouts will be beautifully abundant.

"The steps of a good man are ordered by the Lord" (Psalm 37:23). A hint to the wise is sufficient.

It Pays to Listen

The destination was Snow Camp, North Carolina, to see an outdoor drama — "Sword of Peace." The grandchildren were visiting, and we wanted to entertain them. Snow Camp is not easy to find, even with a map.

Frances Campbell, a knowledgeable friend, called to give us directions. My wife answered the phone and wrote the directions on a piece of folded paper. I read only half, not knowing the rest was on the other side. The map showed a different way.

We passed a sign which said, "Jones Ferry Road." My wife said, "Frances said to turn on Jones' Ferry Road." I said, "You didn't write that down." I followed the map. Driving with that" don't know where you're going" feeling, we finally got there, after going many unnecessary miles.

After the drama, we started back. I just knew I remembered the turns. I did—except one. A sign said "To-85," pointing left. Harriett said that was the way. My superior wisdom said, "That goes toward Greensboro; we want to go toward Chapel Hill." I turned right. Things didn't look familiar. Several miles down the road, a highway marker said S.R. 1005. I knew we were supposed to be on S.R. 1004; but shoot, that's only one number's difference.

Now the only difference in the two numbers is one goes toward Chapel Hill, the other to Siler City—a far piece from our Durham destination. I hadn't seen Siler City at night for a long time. I saw it that night, with my laughing wife by my side.

The grandchildren wanted a Hardee's hamburger, but the place was closing just as we got there. My night got darker. I reckon I apologized half a dozen times; and, with chagrin, admitted my stupidity for not listening to someone who knew better than I.

Upon our midnight arrival home, the first thing my wife did was hand me the paper with the directions on it. Unfolded, it plainly read, "Turn on Jones' Ferry Road."

"But I hadn't read that side," I protested. Her silent response didn't help much. Her forgiving spirit did.

Next morning, Frances called to see if we found Snow Camp all right. I explained every dumb turn I had taken, took all the blame, and awaited a verdict, like a caught crook admitting his guilt in court. "That just shows that women are smarter than men," she said, with calm politeness.

I've decided when my wife says turn left, I will. If it's turn right, right it will be. If she names a road, I'll check it out. I ate enough humble pie that night to last a long time.

The Bible says, "Thine ears shall hear a word behind thee, saying, 'This is the way, walk ye in it, when ye turn to the right hand, and when ye turn to the left' " (Isaiah 30:21).

God's directions are better guides than our bull-headed instincts. He knows the right way. Following His directions will keep us from some unplanned destination in the blackness of night. Cuts down on embarrassment, too.

A Fuelish Story

Little cars never run out of gas. Right? Wrong. It all depends on the driver. The gas tank is more like a cistern than an artesian well. And cisterns do run dry.

My Ford Fiesta was a running piece of machinery. Being an economy car, it seemed as if it ought to run a long, long way on a little bit of gas. It did, but I discovered it had its limits.

The fuel gauge had a thoughtful touch on it, kind of a silent warning. When the needle pointed to the orange zone, the tank was singing, "How Dry I Am." Being unfamiliar with its ways, I figured it meant there's a gallon or so left. I kept going. Turned out to be like trying to go through a caution light that turns red just before you get there, with a cop watching.

On an usually busy thoroughfare, the Fiesta took a siesta. More than that, it just plain died. Fortunately, a station was ahead on the left. Whipping across the road and going down the shoulder, I coasted right up to the pump. Trying to make it on an empty tank could have spelled tragedy.

At a later time, I pushed my luck again. Knowing the tank was as dry as a desert tramp's canteen with one swallow left, I headed for the station. It took nine-and-nine-tenths gallons to fill the ten gallon tank. That's what you call just barely making it. It was one of those "whew!" situations.

On other occasions, I use the common sense God gave me by keeping the tank well-filled. It sure eases your mind to know you've made ample preparation to reach your destination. Makes good sense, too.

This "fuelish" story has its counterpart in the spiritual realm.

The man whose life is not filled with Jesus is sure to play out in the middle of life's highway. Unlike the Fiesta, he can't coast to a "filling station." The Bible knows nothing of salvation on yon side of the grave. It does say, "How shall we escape if we neglect so great salvation?" (Hebrews 2:3). It's a picture of the empty life.

Again, some folks cut it mighty close. A seventy-six-year-old man confessed that he did not know the Lord. After sharing the message of God's love with him, I asked if he would be willing to ask Jesus to come into his heart. He said, "No, I think I'll leave it like it is." He had about a tenth of a "gallon" left. But, like the thief on the cross, he could hope to be able to say before too late, "Lord, remember me when Thou comest into Thy kingdom" (Luke 23:42). That's risky business, though.

Then there are those who "fill up" early in life. They are the ones in whose hearts Christ dwells by faith (Ephesians 3:17). His desire for them is "That ye might be filled with all the fullness of God" (Ephesians 3:19). That life will never run dry.

Better "fill 'er up."

Condemned or Commended?

"Civil authorities are not a terror to good conduct but to bad behavior. Would you have no dread of him who is in authority? Then do what is right and you will receive his approval and commendation" (Romans 13:3, Amplified New Testament). That's Bible talk for, "Law-abiding folks don't need to be scared of the police."

The old license sticker used up its usefulness at midnight February 15. To be caught showing it thereafter was like saying "Come and get me." The men-of-the-badge would oblige. Avoiding the rush, I had bought my new tag about a month in advance. I was in good shape—except.

That "except" means the tag was in a soup tureen where important papers are kept and not on the car. My intent was to legalize my machine by the last day. The forgetter in my skull was in working order, so I drove to the church on February 16, sporting an emblem that said, "law-breaker's a-driving, law-breaker's a-driving!" Fortunately, luck prevailed.

My thoughtful wife rang me up to remind me of my predicament which could have grave consequences. Telling her I could get back home without getting caught, I was ready to run the risk. Her advice not to try it was more Christian; so son Mark fetched me the new tag. Suddenly legality was my status. The law-breaking reverend was no more.

There's a heap of difference in how you stand on the law. Now that my car was properly decked out, my route home changed. I had intended using streets not so readily patrolled by the cars with blue-flashing lights. Instead, I drove right past the police station and waved at two officers getting into their cruiser. Real bold. Even drove slowly and hoped they would see my car's rear end with the grinning little sticker. For all they would know, it had been there a month. We were on the same side and not enemies at all. Keeping the law works that way.

There's a solemn similarity between our relationship to the law and to Jesus. It makes a whopping difference. The Lord Himself said, "He that believeth on the Son hath everlasting life: and he that believeth not the Son shall not see life; but the wrath of God abideth on him" (John 3:36). Being on His side makes us His friend, and we don't dread His knowing what we do.

Seeing as how we've got to take a trip through life, we'd better do it with the One who knows the rules. He keeps us straight.

Seeing May Be Deceiving

An innocent thing can happen in the wrong place and make the victim look as guilty as a kid caught with his hand in the cookie jar.

Melinda Couch was to meet some folks at the beauty parlor. She walked from where she works. Upon arriving, she was asked if she walked all the way. Her replay sounded a little strange: "I walked part of the way and rolled part of the way." What she meant was she had fallen.

Now falling is bad and embarrassing, but where you fall can make folks jump to the wrong conclusion. The hapless lass had hit the sidewalk right in front of the "likker" store. There she was, rolling around like somebody with a snout full but as sober as a non-drinking judge. Aroused some concern, too. "You all right, lady?" shouted a passing motorist. She was, but her pride and ladyhood were as bruised as a hammered thumb. Good thing she wasn't hiccuping or bleary-eyed from a sleepless night. Her credibility could have been jeopardized. An apt piece of Scripture says, "Let him that thinketh he standeth take heed lest he fall" (1 Corinthians 10:12).

Another easily misjudged story unfolded years ago. His nickname was Foxy, a devout church member who hated whiskey like a moonshiner hates the ax of a law man. Time came when the A.B.C. store was opened in his town. Being as curious as an IRS Agent, he went to the opening, just to see who would be in the crowd.

Now things don't always go as we plan. Foxy was about fence-post wide, usually wore a black suit and always wore a black, broad-brimmed hat. Like King Saul of Israel, "From his shoulders and upward he was higher than any of the people" (1 Samuel 9:2).

Since it was a newsworthy happening, the picture-taking man was there. Sure enough, the grand opening was spread across the newspaper with you-know-who showing above them all. It was a grand slam against one who was "anti" who seemed to be "pro." Foxy was out-foxed by ol' Scratch who loves to trap well-meaning folks into compromising positions.

I reckon all of us have been in those "'taint so" situations. It's comforting to know, though, "Man looketh on the outward appearance, the Lord looketh on the heart" (1 Samuel 16:7). Self-appointed judges may have a hey-day in the court of public opinion in witnessing to what they saw, but truth is the bailiwick of the Righteous Judge in whose hands we rest our case.

Our best defense against being wrongly accused is to consistently "live soberly, righteously and godly in the present world" (Titus 2:12). Then some outlandish "Did you see so-and-so?" rumor would be as believable as hearing Chicken Little's frantic cry, "The sky is falling, the sky is falling!"

Whockumjawed

Some words grab your mind like a fish hook. A real doozie was added to my word power to which Mr. Webster's unabridged dictionary didn't build a bridge: "Whockumjawed." Even if you can pronounce it, you feel a need to scratch your head to unravel its mystery.

Had that three-syllable beaut hit me unillustrated, my lower jaw might have hung loose in wonderment. As it was, a right clear picture came through. I had asked a friend how much land he had. In describing the acreage, all four sides measured differently. That's when he said, "It's whockumjawed."

I knew exactly what he meant. The lot was lopsided. It was a corner that had been cut off of what was once a plantation. His home was built on a whockumjawed piece of ground. If you didn't know better, you might worry about his safety.

Now this descriptive word may have theological overtones. None of the new versions of Scripture has incorporated it, but a passel of Bible folk are examples of it. God intended a proper balance between the temporal and eternal, with a sizable amount of leaning toward the eternal. That's what you called good lopsideness. Leaning too far toward the temporal causes a bad case of the wrong kind of whockumjaws can be fatal.

King Solomon started out very well. He rode into town, real humble-like, on a mule. God showered him with an abundance of wealth and wisdom. Ruled for forty years in greatness. But the Bible says he "loved many strange women" —a thousand of them of which God said, "Thou shalt not." Sure put his renowned wisdom in jeopardy. Alas, "His wives turned away his heart after other gods: and his heart was not perfect with the Lord his God" (1 Kings 11:4). In his old age, he got whockumjawed in the bad sense.

Jesus told of a farmer who produced more crops than he could handle. Figured on bigger barns and a long life of plenty. Gonna have fun. "But God said unto him, Thou fool, this night thy soul shall be required of thee" (Luke 12:20). Did he evermore go down with the fool kind of whockumjaws!

Lots of foolish folks mistakenly put all their stock in the earthly life and are as lopsided as a house about to fall. But happy are those saved folks who lay up treasure in heaven and sing "I'd rather have Jesus than anything!" They're "Leaning on Jesus, leaning on Jesus, safe and secure from all alarm!"

If we're wockumjawed toward Jesus, we may look lopsided to the world; but we're leaning just right. Just right.

When Wires Get Crossed

Things, tangled up, produce odd results. We can extract life-lessons from them.

Cliff Price takes walks on a treadmill. The scenery remains the same, but it's profitable for the body, soul, and spirit; a tonic for the whole person.

His "moving sidewalk" is equipped with an electronic gizmo that clips onto the ear lobe. Gives a read-out of how fast the heart is beating. It's kinda like a space-age stethoscope.

Evidently, Cliff had walked as far as he cared to and decided wife Lib should take a stroll. The pace is slow at first, gradually increasing both speed and angle to raise the heartbeat level. The greater the effort, the greater the benefit.

Something wasn't right. Lib was huffing and puffing, like a train pulling a steep grade, but the heartbeat had gained no momentum. Turn up the power, get that ticker ticking! Just before she was about to cave in, she yelled for Cliff to stop that monster.

A moment of truth had arrived. The heartbeat-counter was still on *his* ear lobe instead of hers! Poor Lib wondered how she traveled so fast, got so out of breath and yet her heart stayed in low gear instead of overdrive. If she ever gets on that thing again, she'll probably be singing, "I'd rather do it my way." Laughingly, it got all straightened out.

From this experience, a few life-applications may tread into our minds.

Life can get pretty hectic because someone gets his wires crossed. A friendship may be greatly strained due to misunderstanding, a lie, harsh gossip, a burst of anger. But how happy when the wires get uncrossed and friends are friends again!

And another: it pays to listen to our own heart. Having its own language, that little critter might beat out a love song. The right hookup enables it to beat in rhythm with God's love. Jesus is the connection.

Then again, when one person tries to control another's walk, undue stress sets in, creating bondage and weariness. Finally, the inner voice of liberty cries, "Whoa! That's enough!" Then we get off of somebody else's treadmill and discover God's way for our life. It's freedom to follow God's call and to hear this: "Thine ears shall hear a word behind thee, saying, This is the way, walk ye in it" (Isaiah 30:21). And it becomes our God-willed pathway.

Like the old hymn has it, "When we walk with the Lord, in the light of His word, what a glory He sheds our way!"

Life with Jesus is not a treadmill. It goes somewhere.

On Gullibility

All comedy is not found on the comic page of the newspaper. And so-called facts sometime turn out to be pure fiction.

A humdinger appeared in the paper. Somebody had discovered a fossilized egg, calculated to be 16,000,000 years old. Why, that even goes back before Columbus lucked up on America. They didn't say what kind of critter laid the egg, and the egg wouldn't tell either. To say the least, it sure was hard boiled.

Mistakes have a way of being exposed. New evidence showed the supposed fossil to probably be a mammal stomach stone. Most likely from a cow. Maybe her cud slipped down her throat and hardened. It was thought to have been in the ground maybe three to five years. Now it's something when highly educated folks can't tell the difference between an egg and something from a cow's storage bin. Udderly amazing!

Let's see now: 5 years from 16,000,000 is 15,999,995. Given the benefit of the doubt, they didn't miss it by much. The value of the find (?) must have decreased considerably. Anyhow, it's heartening to know the real brainy can "flub-the-dub" as well as us minimal-minded folks.

And things aren't always what they appear to be, either. The above fiasco jogged a certain memory to the surface. It's about our boys when they were growing up.

Russell, the younger, got a telescope for Christmas. He scanned the heavens as far as the rather puny scope would fetch objects into view.

With a note of excitement, he called his brother, Mark, to come look at his heavenly-body discovery. Seeing possible craters and maybe a face, Mark determined it was the moon. A momentous moment. It seemed the moon was real close to earth.

It was. In fact, right across the street. Russell had trained the telescope on the neighbor's basketball backboard. Painted white, with chips and scratches which resembled craters and illuminated by the street light, it appeared to be the silvery moon.

Poor Mark was the butt of a joke. Took it good naturedly. Even laughed with the guffawing young

"Galileo" who had caused him to appear moonstruck. To this day, they still remain as close-knit as two brothers can be.

Guess it just shows that all of us get fooled at times. It's called gullibility. It pays to be able to laugh at ourselves. Better to grin and bear it, than to blow a gasket and get all heated up. Like the old saying, "Smile and the world smiles with you; frown and you frown alone."

No one is as smart as he thinks he is. The Bible says, "A man ought not to think more highly of himself than he ought to think" (Romans 12:3). Maybe a more humble and realistic opinion of ourselves would make us more tolerable and less brassy.

A Parable with Wings

My flying friend, Stuart Henderson, is the source of another parable with wings.

He decided to put his little Citabria through its paces. Fortunately, the air space was over and around the area where the plane is hangared.

During loops, split eights and snap-rolls, the engine was as rough as a sore throat. Throttle adjustment made no difference. Wisely, Ace landed. A friend informed him of the black smoke with which the flying machine had been polluting the air.

Stuart's intelligence shone brightly when he refused to fly again until a mechanic checked it out. A hairline crack was found in the carburetor float. The faulty carb was removed, rebuilt and re-installed.

Five hundred bucks sounded reasonable when what might have happened was considered. Stuart could've looked like one of those little critters that started across the highway and didn't make it. We both agreed that the good Lord was flying with him. (And I was glad that I had been a spectator from the ground instead of an air-sick passenger up yonder.)

With the renewed part in place, the plane checked out perfectly. Acrobatics could be executed (pardon the term) with confidence and without fear to those who are inclined to twist, turn, and roll over in the wide blue yonder. Stuart's good judgment paid off.

It's kind of like life, when viewed from the Christian perspective.

Many a person flies along, cutting all kinds of shines. He may sense that something isn't just right, not knowing that his spiritual float is cracked. The black smoke he emits pollutes his world, but danger of destruction hasn't set in yet. Without knowing it, he stays up only by the grace of God.

Finally, conviction to land for inspection flies into his mind. Determination to find the trouble keeps him from risking his immortal soul any longer.

The soul expert, Jesus, is called upon. Doesn't take Him any time to diagnose the trouble. Everyone has "engine trouble." It's called fallen nature. Sooner or later it causes a person to crack up. It's being lost as opposed to being saved.

Unlike getting an overhaul, the Lord gives us a new nature. The Bible declares, "If any man be in Christ, he is a new creation: old things are passed away; behold, all things are become new" (2 Corinthians 5:17).

When the new engine is revved up, we take off in a different direction, soar higher than ever before, and even do some pretty fancy things that get God's smile of approval.

No need to worry about falling, for "He is able to keep you from falling" (Jude 24). And when we've flown out our time, we can joyfully sing "I'll fly away, O glory, I'll away" *to* glory.

It's a Matter of Taste

One slip can undo a lifetime of good. Here's a tale that's food for thought.

A delicious chicken dinner had been enjoyed. The chicken portion had "entered the ministry." The jumbo, buttered, sour-creamed, cheesed, baked potato and Texas toast had been washed down with cold tea. Gave you that satisfied feeling, leaving a good taste in the mouth.

At the paying place was a dish of mints, with various flavors in the centers. They are free, designed to sort of cap off the meal. My wife gave me one, not noticing which kind.

Out of all the flavors, the one I popped into my mouth raised the hackles on my taste buds. Licorice! Now I reckon there are folks who can tolerate such a taste and some even like it. I'm about as fond of licorice as Dennis the Menace is of carrots.

After cutting down on that supposedly refreshing morsel, it had to go. Once outside, I spit that thing as far as my spitter would send it. Gone it was, but the effects lingered. Gone, too, was that fine chicken-dinner taste. All I could taste was licorice. Just about ruined my meal.

History is replete with sad accounts of how one wrong choice can change the taste of life from then on.

Adam and Eve found that one bite of the forbidden fruit didn't come close to tasting like apple pie. It ruined Paradise for them and us. The world has had the taste of sin in it ever since.

One act of King David as a Peeping Tom fostered multiple shameful consequences. It left a dark taste of regret in his life that he never really got over.

Many a rising-star politician has had his stardust turn to dust by one time getting caught with his sticky fingers in the till under the counter. He knows the taste of ashes.

Even preachers have been de-preacherized through a one-time moral flop. Suddenly the sweet taste of God's blessings turned sour.

A one time misunderstanding can turn a beautiful friendship into ugliness. Bitterness is the accompanying taste. It even alters the countenance and turns the corners of the mouth down.

A hurtful word, hastily spoken, often destroys a relationship that was a joy of long duration. Just a word. A cutting one. Leaves the taste of tears in its wake.

The secret of the whole matter is to be on guard against the unguarded moment. Wise ol' Solomon warned, "Whoso diggeth a pit shall fall therein" (Proverbs 26:27).

One way to stay out of the "pit" is to know the difference between chicken and licorice. Could make a tasty difference, for life.

Two Kinds of Potholes

Early winter of '89 had some days that were real doozies. Before it arrived officially on the 21st, North Pole weather smacked the South broadside. Lord Temperature got up a courtship with Lady Freeze and took an excursion in the vicinity of The Land of Zero.

Some things don't fare too well when it's as cold as all get out. Like highways. On a stretch of I-85, betwixt Durham and Greensboro, North Carolina, a big flashing sign read, "Reduce speed next 23 miles," and for good reason.

The Potholer had come out of hiding and popped out chunks of asphalt for a fare-you-well. He created big potholes, little potholes and sizes in between. Looked like big ol' chicken pox scars on the highway's face.

Driving that 23 miles was like being on an obstacle course. In spite of everything, I'd hit some potholes. The poor car would give a painful cry of "thud-clunk"; the passenger's false teeth would rattle. I could no more miss all of those potholes than I could build a Southern snowman in July.

But something nice took place. A couple of days later, I made the same trip. There was evidence the pothole fixer had been fixin'. Low-and-behold, I didn't have to dart about like trying to avoid a drunk driver.

Made a person mighty thankful for those unknown, unsung heroes who had de-potholed the road. Even the car seemed grateful, and false teeth rattled no more.

Admittedly, this highway yarn is as full of holes as Swiss cheese, but its counterpart is life itself. Folks have to contend with such a variety of potholes it makes 23 miles of pock-marked road seem like walking around the block.

To name a few of these thuddy places may encourage seeking the One who can fill them, seeing as how they make life a pretty jolting journey.

There are unwanted potholes of depression, loneliness, grief, a sense of failure. Then, times not a few, the chief pothole maker, Satan, tears up the heart's highway with ragged holes of hatred, lying, lust, greed, vengeance, bad habits, hair-trigger temper, bitterness, or some other soul-jarring sin.

But there's good news. Jesus came to fill the rough places in our lives with His forgiveness, love, and peace. He fulfills the promise, "A highway will be there; it will be called The Way of Holiness." And for those who travel it, "gladness and joy will overtake them, and sorrow and sighing will flee away" (Isaiah 35:8, 10, NIV.).

There's not a "pothole" Jesus can't fix. For in Him, "the rough ground shall become level, the rugged places a plain" (Isaiah 40:4, NIV).

Foiling the Sock Monster

Somewhere between the dirty clothes hamper, the washing machine, and the dryer lurks the sock monster. He has neither form nor substance, but he's more real than Big Foot. Since he's as evasive as a crook on the lam, no one has ever seen him. He's a master at thieving and aggravation.

This ghostly creature has an insatiable appetite for socks. Funny thing, though, he will not devour a pair of socks. He eats only one, leaving the mate to face loneliness and uselessness in some dresser drawer. Gradually that one is joined by other orphaned socks, getting as tangled as unrolled yarn.

After searching, trying to match one with another that won't match and hoping the mystery of the missing sock will be solved, discard time comes. Many a time, perfectly good socks, with neither hole nor run, end up in a rag bag or in a shine box.

Now no one in the family wants to take the blame for who did what with the vanished sock. And the sock monster giggles and burps.

Hold on now. Good news for all who have faced these disconcerting frustrations. The sock monster faces a new wrinkle that will either make him eat a pair at a time or disappear altogether.

My wife devised a scheme that is so simple, takes hardly any time, that should bring peace to many a household. May even cut down on the divorce rate.

She emptied the sock drawer, matched up every pair that had a mate and pinned each pair at the toe with a safety pin. Even in the dark you can extract a pair of socks, without giving it a second thought.

A week or two later, when it's time to change socks, the pin is removed from the clean ones and inserted in the toes of the slightly soiled ones. When the sock monster chomps down on that pin, it breaks his teeth, and he spits the pinned pair out. He sulks, hoping that by some twist of fate another single will come along. In the meantime, every pair of socks has made the complete cycle, without losing half of itself along the way.

One word of caution: be sure to unpin the socks before putting them on or else you're apt to fall on your kisser when you try to walk. Few systems are absolutely fool proof, but this one has great merit.

I predict that harmony will return to couples galore, the safety pin industry will thrive, and socks will live happily everafter in togetherness.

Fare-thee-well, sock monster; you're no match for this "socker match."

The Bible assures "He that handleth a matter wisely shall find good" (Proverbs 16:20). Verily, 'tis so.

Dewrathing Wrath

"Let not the sun go down upon your wrath" (Ephesians 4:26). That means get your differences settled immediately, if not sooner. Smoldering anger can get inferno big, if enough fuel is added. The good Lord knows this, so He told us to stomp out the fire before sundown.

I read about a young fellow who would've been a sight better off if he had banked his fire instead of stoking it.

An argument at a 7-11 Store was over a two-cent charge for a book of matches. The disgruntled customer left without paying. Police officers saw him leave, and the chase was on. Trying to elude his pursuers made him do a right stupid thing.

He drove his two-year-old sports car up a railroad embankment and got stuck on the tracks. He fled, but not far. From the custodial back seat of the police cruiser, he watched a freight train total his beloved machine. Got himself booked for reckless driving and attempting to elude the police. I reckon he felt like two cents.

Similar shenanigans have left a trail of destruction since Cain wrathfully rose up against his brother Abel and slew him (Genesis 4:8). Like those who have followed in his train, he probably wished the sun hadn't set so soon that day.

The fallout of a mad fit can be limited about as easily as putting the ash from an erupted volcano into a tin pail.

Since the verse says "let not," some control over our actions is implied. We don't have much "sayso" as to when ol' Sol is going to set, but the reins of wrath are in our hands. "Let not" means to haul back on the reins and say "Whoa!" It's kind of like stopping a horse that's about to run away.

The connecting verse says, "Neither give place to the devil" (Ephesians 4:27). Wrath is as inviting to the devil as fire is to a pyromaniac. We are cautioned to give him no foothold. Take the "d" out of devil and you have "evil." That accurately describes what he will do when our anger-pot boils over.

The Bible says "put away wrath" (Ephesians 4:31). Many a man has been "put away" because he didn't put away his wrath. When excessive anger has given the devil a place to work, the words "I'm sorry" work like magic. Of course, the Lord offers His help to keep us from doing so many devilish things.

Tomorrow's sunrise will seem brighter, if we set things right with man and God before the sun sets today.

Quality Control Pays

"A bird in the hand is worth two in a bush." That may make sense to a hunter, but a bird in a vat of toothpaste is another story.

A news item reported a quality control check at a Gleem toothpaste-making company revealed the remains of a bird in 180,000 pounds of the tooth-cleaning, breath-sweetening concoction. For fear that users might develop "feathery mouth," the whole batch had to be hauled to a landfill and the system flushed fifteen times. The landfill never "gleamed" like that before.

Now one poor little bird, whose species was undeterminable, had, with neither malice nor forethought, caused a heap of trouble. He had about as much intention of such a pasty demise as he had of gleaming his beak with the gooey stuff. No one knew how it happened, but it's a tough way to get yourself in the news.

Consider the loss incurred: 180,000 pounds is 2,880,000 ounces. That's 450,000 tubes of 6.4 ounces of toothpaste. At a conservative estimate of 40 squirts per tube, that's 18,000,000 times when somebody's mouth could have been improved. And that's about 7 percent of the U.S. population getting just one brushing per citizen. At two bucks a tube, $900,000 went the way of the gooney bird.

To its credit, the company did right in getting rid of the contamination, lest it spread to where only the Lord knows.

This bird-in-the-toothpaste story illustrates something the Bible says that is as true today as when first uttered. "A little leaven leaveneth the whole lump" (1 Corinthians 5:6).

Leaven is yeast, which permeates dough, making it rise. In the Bible, the word is often used to describe how evil works. A little pinch of sin wreaks havoc in a person's life all out of proportion to its size. (Like a few ounces of bird in 180,000 pounds of toothpaste.)

Look at some "bird remains" that cause ruination. A puff of marijuana can lead to a lifetime of drug addiction, and that first drink can lead to alcoholism. Both of these destroy body, mind, and soul. Lustful thoughts can lead to adultery, which kills marriages. A little "white" lie can lead to a loss of honor. Unchecked anger can lead to murder. A little gossip can destroy someone's reputation. Jealousy may become a green-eyed monster. Envy can lead to financial ruin.

Quality control means inspection; inspection should lead to correction. Our personal "vats" need the removal of discovered pollutants and the flushing of our inner selves by the Holy Spirit. The Bible gives instructions for the process: "Purge out the old leaven, that ye may be a new lump" (1 Corinthians 5:7). And the world could use some "new lump" Christians.

The purging place is found at the foot of the cross: Christ will meet you there. He knows how to clean the heart of all impurities, replacing them with a desire to live an uncontaminated life. It's called quality control.

Environmental pollution is bad enough; inner pollution is worse. Jesus puts a "gleam" in us and shines through our lives.

Confession Can Be Therapeutic

In his straightforward Epistle, James says, "Confess your faults one to another, and pray for one another" (James 5:16). In the context of the passage, he is talking about healing. There's another possible application of the advice. It has to do with identifying with the human race. Admitting our imperfections and our need for somebody to pray for us, lowers the ego level considerably.

Here goes a public confession of an event that nobody knew about at the time except me and the good Lord. Mercifully, He keeps our secrets; but to confess my active proneness toward stupidity may encourage some other pilgrim to shout, "Me, too!"

I had retrieved our television set from the repair shop, and placed it on the car's front seat where its white cabinet made it visible. I needed to do some shopping, and the thought crossed my mind that some passerbys might be about as honest as Jesse James.

Before entering the store, I got a couple of plastic bags from the trunk of the car and carefully covered the TV. Pushing the electric door lock button, I secured the car's contents.

When my shopping spree was complete, my eyes bugged somewhat as I approached the car. To my chagrin, I discovered that I had left the driver's side door standing wide open. And I do mean wide. It was locked, but a locked, open door would deter a thief about as much as a hole in a roof would keep the rain out.

Some guardian angel must have been assigned to that spot in the parking lot. I surmised that no Jesse James type had happened by. If perchance one did, he missed a golden opportunity to get a TV at a very reasonable price. "O give thanks unto the Lord" seemed the appropriate thing to do. I did.

Admitting to having done some rather dumb things makes Christians more believable. (Other folks, too.) Putting on the air of faultlessness is like a skunk pretending his dispersed "perfume" is Chanel #5.

The Bible warns every person "not to think of himself more highly than he ought to think" (Romans 12:3). If he does, he may find the atmosphere around his self-constructed throne is pretty thin. Gets lonely up there, too.

Telling on oneself has therapeutic values. It deflates a swollen ego like sticking a hatpin in a balloon. It engenders a smattering of compassion toward some other brother who "left his locked door standing open." And it makes others more willing to accept us as the fallible folks that we are—and feel more at ease around us.

Maybe it has something to do with credibility.

SECTION 3

The Tongue Tattles

Word Power

Words are powerful. They can make a person soar with eagle wings or make his feathers droop.

Eleven-year-old Valerie came bouncing home from the orthodontist. She said, "Mama, the doctor bragged on me; told me how good I was and how well I was doing with my braces. The nurse bragged on me, too!"

Speaking without thinking, her mother responded, "I guess they say that to all the little children."

Feathers drooped. The hurt little one despondently said, "Well, Mama. I was feeling pretty good about myself for about five minutes, and you blew it."

Her mama had to redeem herself with an apology and explanation, for it wasn't her intention to be a feather drooper. Wasn't long before soaring wings were back.

There's a cup somewhere deep inside of everybody that longs to have a little praise poured into it. Tastes good. When that cup is left empty, the spirit remains desert thirsty.

Solomon said, "A word fitly spoken is like apples of gold in pictures of silver" (Proverbs 25:11). There's a difference in a word spoken in some kind of fit and a word fitly spoken. One casts down, the other lifts.

What we pour into somebody else's cup should be the same kind of stuff we want poured into ours. It's the Golden Rule rule.

When I was a young preacher, with a lot of learning to do, E.N. Johnson, an older preacher friend, put his arm around my shoulder and said, "Boy, I still believe in you." I think he thought I had possibilities. He's gone, but his words are still in my "cup," often making it run over. I never wanted to disappoint him.

Another time my cup got poured into by nephew David Fore. He was a just a child. At the close of a worship service, I was greeting the people at the door. The only comment I recall from that day was David's: "Crate, that was a good preach." Bless his little heart.

Many are the times my feathers have drooped after a sermon. But I can always remember that at least, in the eyes of a little boy, one time I did a fair job. It still tastes good.

Jesus was always saying good things to people. Things like "Thy sins be forgiven thee," "Go and sin no more," "Love one another as I have loved you," "My peace I give unto you," "Let not your heart be troubled," and a host of other lifting words. My, what thirst quenchers!

Of Jesus it was said, they "wondered at the gracious words which proceeded out of His mouth" (Luke 4:22).

Folks ought to wonder at ours, too.

Togetherness

Lori Jones is a home economics teacher. Upon entering her chosen profession, she had a one year contract while the regular teacher was on leave.

She enjoyed her students, and their good relationship was illustrated in an unexpected way.

A junior high boy informed her that he had enjoyed her class so much that he had signed up for the next year.

Real disappointment was expressed upon being told she was not returning. He said, "Well, Mrs. Jones, then I'll just have to unroll."

Further admiration was evident, when he added, "We've gotten attached to each other. We're just like fleas." Puzzled, she tried to interpret. "You mean it's like I'm the mama flea and you are the baby fleas?" "Naw," he corrected, "It's like you're the dog and we're the fleas."

Ordinarily, being likened to a dog is not the highest compliment. This was the exception. Lori wasn't offended but felt loved and wanted.

A flea has an attachment to a dog that just won't quit. He'll go wherever his chosen friend goes and hang on for dear life. In the canine world, it's often pure agitation and irritation; but, the point of this story is togetherness.

Because the boy loved his teacher, he wanted to be with her. Without her, the course lost its appeal. He made a stab at paying her a compliment, albeit falling a bit short of the intended goal. The analogy said more than he meant, seeing as how students and teachers sometimes irritate one another; but not always. Usually they become attached to one another.

Sometimes an intended compliment is as puzzling as a jigsaw puzzle, but you know there's something beautiful in it.

Now overall, if you scratch around in the conversation, there's an application to marriage.

Tying the knot at a wedding is meant to produce togetherness. The Bible says, "They two shall become one" (Ephesians 5:31). That's about as together as you can get.

Wanting to be together is as natural as a magnet drawing iron. The prospect of a long separation saddens the heart. The faithful husband says, "If I can't be with the one I love, I'll not be with anyone else." Ditto the wife.

Now, in all honesty, folks who live together in holy wedlock have to admit there are times when they irritate each other, but not all the time.

I've heard of folks who say they've lived together for so many years and have never had a cross word. To myself I say, "Hmph. If that's the truth, one can't hear and the other can't talk." Shucks, when you have a spat, you get to kiss and make up. (The wife gets the kiss and the husband gets the makeup.)

Jesus said, "What God has joined together, let no man separate" (Matthew 19:6 NIV).

That's togetherness that enables a man to say, "Honeybunch, we won't ever unroll!"

Truth Won't Stretch

Truth. Jesus said to Pilate, "Everyone that is of the truth heareth My voice," and Pilate retorted, "What is truth?" (John 18:37-38). Truth is an absolute—the opposite of false. Some things are unalterably so—like laws that govern the universe.

Now when truth gets in man's hands, it becomes pliable. It can be told, stretched, twisted, or hidden. Sometimes it's as disguised as a man wearing makeup and a woman's wig. Downright unrecognizable.

Though indestructible, there are times when it is as hard to extract as an impacted wisdom tooth.

An accepted practice is the stretching of truth. Acceptable, that is, among practitioners, but must surely earn a frown from the Lord. We have ways of telling things that are true to a point but are not the whole truth.

Here's a variation of a story I heard. A family wondered what to inscribe in the family Bible about a relative's death. He had swung into eternity at the end of a rope for horse stealing. Didn't seem proper to inform posterity of such a dramatic exit, so discretion was used. "He died from an agonizing, incurable pain in the neck." That he did, but you'll have to agree that something besides the poor guy's neck was stretched. The inscription will most probably be re-translated in the day when falsehood is on the scaffold and Truth is on the throne.

Then there are times when you can tell the truth without telling everything you know. Depends on the question.

One morning a preacher friend stayed in bed longer than he was expected to. The phone rang. Fortunately, the thing was beside the bed. "Did I get you up?" said a suspicious voice. "No," he replied. "You didn't get me up." And he lay right there and conversed. Sounded like he'd been up for hours. Saw no reason to say more than he was asked. He wasn't about to let somebody hang a guilty conscience on him for not greeting the dawn.

Beware, though, truth has a way of working itself into view like weeds growin' through asphalt. Takes a while. Jesus said, "For there is nothing covered, that

51

shall not be revealed; neither hid, that shall not be known. Therefore whatsoever ye have spoken in darkness shall be heard in the light; and that which ye have spoken in the ear in closets shall be proclaimed upon the housetops" (Luke 12:2-3).

Witnesses in court swear on the Bible to tell the whole truth. Sometimes their stories are about as much alike as a giraffe and a donkey. The judge finally decides who's got a handle on truth.

We ought to so live that when Station T-R-U-T-H broadcasts from the housetop, there'll be no shame as we stand before the "Judge of all earth."

Word Pictures

The right choice of words is vital and sometimes tricky. Words create pictures. A speaker had better beware lest his words put his audience to thinking something he never intended.

Dr. V. L. Stanfield, my preaching professor at Southern Seminary, told how the point of a good story can become a fork in the road. In a sermon on the prodigal son (Luke 15), the preacher was describing the glad homecoming: "When the father saw his son coming down the road, he ran like a streak of lightning and grabbed him around the neck." That's a right electrifying scene of a family reunion. What the Bible really says is, "His father saw him, and had compassion, and ran, and fell on his neck, and kissed him" (Luke 15:20). The preacher embellished it a tad.

At that point, Dr. Stanfield's mind took off in another direction. He said, "I could just imagine what happened to the boy when his father grabbed him at that speed." The thought of such a neck-poppin' welcome tended to turn a grand old story into a mental comedy. Anyway, it was hard to meditate on the love of the Father for thinking about the wandering boy's return getting him hit like a bolt out of the blue.

I remember hearing about an outline of a message on the story of the Prodigal Son:

I. He lost his shirt

II. He lost his undershirt

III. Then he came to himself

Admittedly, those are the bare facts of the story, for it says, "He wasted his substance in riotous living...he spent all...and he came to himself" (Luke 15:13-14,17). But the aim of the account has more to do with the robe they put on him than the shirt he lost.

Vivid, picturesque preaching can be as persuasive as a politician courtin' votes. One preacher stoked the fires of the bad place real good by saying, "Hell is seven times hotter than the hottest furnace." An impressed but skeptical hearer said, "I don't know, Preacher; I don't believe a man's constitution could stand that!" Maybe not, but it sure makes finding out risky. Jesus said one of hell's residents cried, "I am tormented in this flame!" (Luke 16:24). Makes hell a place to be shunned like the plague.

One the other hand, John tells of heaven's being a place where God is with His people. Says he: "And God shall wipe away all tears from their eyes; and there shall be no more death, neither sorrow, nor crying, neither shall there be any more pain...There shall be no night there" (Revelation 21:4, 25). What a picture! Makes a fellow want to go with the next load they're getting up!

When word-windows are undistorted, you don't have to squint to see the pictures through them.

Mouthing

"**S**et a watch, O Lord, before my mouth; keep the door of my lips" (Psalm 141:3). David was honest enough to admit his sins and weaknesses. He comes through as a friend we can trust. Like the rest of us, he must've had trouble at times keeping his trap shut. So he called for help. The memory of things said that should've died in the thinking stage probably troubled him.

Some of us are like a little fellow I saw. He was doing more than his share of talking. His mama wanted relief from the barrage of words. Told him to hush. Undaunted, he said, "Its my mouth, and I can talk if I want to." Without knowing it, he was paraphrasing Psalm 12:4b: "Our lips are our own: who is Lord over us?" (A statement of defiance.)

Words come in infinite varieties. Long, short, good, bad, soft, loud, sharp, dull, cutting, soothing, insulting, edifying, true, and false. Makes you fell sorry for what a mouth has to contend with. 'Course you can't blame the mouth; it just says what it's told to say.

A mechanic friend ripped out a few bad words—as was his custom (spelled Cusstom). Wearing the hat of a rebuker, I rebuked. Thought it was my duty. His reply was short, justifying the practice. "Makes your stomach feel better." My concern was his soul; his avoiding ulcers. Guess it depends on where a person would rather have ulcers.

Sometimes we have to get to know a person to know how to take what he says. Cheerfully, I said to a friend, "How are you?" His reply didn't exactly please me. "What do you care? You're not a doctor and not much of a preacher." I guess what upset me was I had a sneaking suspicion he was telling the truth. The doctor part didn't bother me; the other part wasn't the nicest thing I had ever heard.

Later I discovered this man had an unusual way of joking. I didn't need to be offended at all. I learned to wade through the words and found a real sensitive heart and a supportive friend. We had many words at the throne of grace together.

Bad situations don't call for bad expressions. Dr. Leo Eddleman, of preaching and teaching fame, said, "One time I hit my thumb with a hammer. I got real mad and lost my temper. I said, 'Umm-umph! Don't it hurt!'" He knew what it was for the Lord to stand guard over his mouth.

The word "watch" can also mean a timepiece. A loose translation of the verse might suggest there are times not to speak. For some of us, the Lord would need to use an alarm clock to make us hush.

Soap Opera

Sometimes, attempts at situation correcting can backfire like an old Model T Ford.

A certain three-year-old picked up a real dirty word. Most likely didn't know its meaning, and most likely came from some adult who did. Anyhow, the word passed form the little fella's ears, through his mouth and landed within earshot of his mama. Uh oh!

Since his was a Christian family and as active in church as a bee in a hive, such language was as out of place as a Smith at a Jones' family reunion. It was time to cut offensive words off at the pass. Mama went into action.

She must've been of the old school, for her method of correction would've put child psychologists into a tailspin. She washed his mouth out with soap. Would you ever! Figured the word was as gone as a burst soap bubble.

No doubt a clear as spring water explanation as to the why of the whole procedure accompanied the act that tasted worse than the dirty word. But the little one didn't quite understand why it didn't work.

Good-intentioned Mama, whose motive was to help her boy talk nice, was faced with a puzzling question. A question about as easy to answer as trying to explain why green soap makes white suds. "Mama, you washed my mouth out with soap, but it didn't take the word out. I can still say the word." He just wondered why.

Now he wasn't trying to be sassy or defiant. Neither was it a threat to run it by again. He honestly had a problem. If soap is supposed to clean things up, why was the word still floating around in his head like a bar of Ivory?

Mama's approach fell a little short of its intended goal. Some things are just too difficult for even an extra-bright three-year-old to understand.

From this "soap opera," entitled "Washout at O.K. Laundromat," a thought or two may be worth considering, such as:

Dirty stuff sticks in the mind like thrown mud on a wall. And it pops up again and again like uninvited company. But filling the mind with good stuff leaves little sticking room for dirt. Crowds it out.

In the comic strip Lil' Abner, there was a sampler on Mammy Yokum's wall: "Good Is Better Than Evil, Because It's Nicer." Right on, Mammy! That's a loose paraphrase of "Whatever is true, honest, just, pure, lovely, and of good report; think on these things" (Phillippians 4:8).

Psalm writer, David, has given us a fine, purifying prayer to pray: "Let the words of my mouth, *and* the meditations of my heart, be acceptable in Thy sight, O Lord, my strength, and my Redeemer" (Psalm 19:14).

Excommunicated for Cussin'

Excuses for quitting church make you question man's intelligence. Being created in God's image, you'd think he'd have sense enough to know he ought to worship his Maker. Alas, the devil kicks the gears of his mind into neutral, and the duped soul descends downhill backwards. Seems to think he's making progress.

A man had run past his three-score-years-and-ten by nearly ten more. That's enough to get real saintly, but he had carried bad feelings against the church. His excuse was a stable one: they kicked him out of the church for cussin' a horse. You might say he didn't bridle his tongue. Had a burr under his saddle from then on.

I reckon this church-eviction took place in the days when cussin' was frowned on. Now days it might be hard to muster up an innocent crowd big enough to vote the offenders out. That doesn't mean the practice is more acceptable. It's just more accepted. A fellow would have to stretch the truth to say he lost his place in the church for laying a cussin' on someone or something. That's one less usable excuse.

'Course, the church hasn't helped herself much in the eyes of the world by ignoring profane members who "blue-streak" the air. The Bible still says, "Out of the same mouth proceedeth blessing and cursing...These things ought not to be" (James 3:10).

Whatever excuse is employed to separate a person from the church makes about as much sense as using a parachute with a cut ripcord. Makes a man critical, self-righteous, bitter, and robs him of all those fine blessings the good Lord just loves to give.

The Bible says, "Christ loved the church, and gave Himself for it" (Ephesians 5:25). Can you imagine why anyone would drum up flimsy excuses to stay apart from what Jesus loves and died for? Better to be like David who said, "I was glad when they said unto me, Let us go into the house of the Lord" (Psalm 122:1).

Don't let the devil give you the horse laugh for using the church-quittin' excuse he handed you.

Garbage from an Inner Dump

All garbage is not in the city or county dumps. There's another kind that can neither be seen nor smelled. If it could be, eyeballs would bulge and nostrils would curl.

This particular kind of garbage assaults the ears and makes you wish for automatic earflaps that would close when a gob of it is coming your way.

It's called profanity, four letter words, filthy language, cursing. It originates in the mind, flows through the mouth, and defiles everything it touches. It has as much value as stump water in a perfume bottle and reveals the values of the "garbage dispenser."

When I was pastor of Angier Avenue Baptist Church, I would cross the street to the Post Office every day to get the church mail. For some reason, doing business there often brought out the worst in people.

A clerk told of his encounter with an irate woman gifted in gutter language. Never in his life had he been cussed like he was cussed that day—and for something not his fault. Being a decent man, he couldn't do a replay. He had laughed at her and said, "I hope you don't eat with the same mouth you talk out of." That was like opening the intake valve at the sewage treatment plant. She drenched him again.

Another time, I was standing in line at the post office when I heard a young woman who had attended my church dumping a truckload of taking God's Name in vain. Her conversation was laced with words you wouldn't think a woman would use.

She evidently had not learned "The Lord will not hold him guiltless that taketh His Name in vain" (Exodus 20:7).

On one occasion, the post office stamp machine refused to cooperate, aggravating a lady customer. She reacted impulsively. Her tongue made a quick descent to the storage room of words and selected a right nasty one.

There was a large, standing-sign between her and me. I wasn't hiding, but I was hidden from her view. Revealing my presence brought a surprised reaction. Knowing that I was a preacher, she was apologetic and flustered. With evident embarrassment, she said, "I didn't know you were there." She probably wished she had left the word unsaid.

My ministerial ears had heard the word before. It isn't the worst there is, but I've never used it in a sermon. To do so would most likely put ruination on my sermonizing.

Our God-given mouths are meant for good words. There's an encouraging word from the Bible to help us remember: "Pleasant words are as a honeycomb, sweet to the soul, and health to the bones" (Proverbs 16:24).

Talk-ee Walk-ee

"**D**on't do as I do; do as I say." That's saying take my advice, but don't follow my example. It implies that what we know is better than what we do. To expect such a stance to bear fruits of righteousness is like expecting peaches from a thorn bush. We are more apt to mimic what we see than obey what we hear.

It was state fair time. Among the many attractions, there's the Midway. Ah, the midway! As magnetic as the North Pole. So a certain precautionary Pop counseled his "fair-headed" impressionable teenager, "Son, stay out of those girlie shows: you might see something you're not supposed to see." That was like telling Brer Rabbit to stay out of the briar patch.

The young fellow went as straight to the forbidden tent as Eve to the forbidden tree. He was in for a real eye-opener. He said, "Sure enough, I saw something I wasn't supposed to see: I saw my daddy." There he was, on the front row, swallowing candy by the handfuls, eyes a-poppin'.

To think anybody will pay much attention to what we say, unless we live accordingly, is wishful thinking. Who would go to a snaggle-toothed dentist or a stringy-haired beautician? Who trusts a mechanic whose own car won't hit a lick? What overweight person would follow the plan of a 317 1/2 pound doctor? Who listens to a preacher who's "agin sin," but whose private life won't stand the light of day? In every case, observers would be saying, "Physician, heal thyself" (Luke 4:23).

Example speaks louder than words. When the two clasp hands, credibility is established. That person's for real.

Jesus is our best reference point. He said, "I have given you an example, that you should do as I have done to you" (John 13:15). His commands and performance were, and are, always a "Command Performance."

Paul learned to walk so in step with Jesus that he could say, "Those things which ye have both learned, and received, and heard, *and seen in me*, do" (Philippians 4:9). The man lived what he said and had earned the right to say, "Do as I do."

Talk the talk and walk the walk is the way to go.

Inner and Outer Ought to Track

Jesus laid some pretty heavy words on folks whose inner and outer lives run counter to each other. Said the One who knows the heart of man, "Ye outwardly appear righteous unto men, but within ye are full of hypocrisy and iniquity" (Matthew 23:28).

That's like a crook wearing his thousand-dollar suit and forgetting that God sees through the threads, leaving him "threadbare."

Inner is of greater importance than outer. Getting them to track gives authenticity to one's life.

Now sometimes too much emphasis can be put on relatively minor, outer things—making the major, inner things obscure.

Like the time a seminary professor was enjoying a cup of coffee in the student center.

Inviting a student to join him in such "drinking," he was met with an unexpected rebuke. "No, thank you," said the young theologue, "I'm a Christian." No doubt, he had a conviction that coffee sipping wasn't compatible with walking with the Lord. The renowned prof's retort may have caused the lad's piety to percolate a little: "I am too, but it didn't make a fool out of me."

Most likely, downing a mug of coffee is not likely to interfere with the process of one's sanctification. Neither is it apt to be an insurmountable hindrance to some soul seeking the Lord.

Seems to me, refusing the offer on the grounds of being subject to coffee-nerves, sleeplessness, or just plain dislike of the stuff would've made more sense. Personally, I doubt that abstinence from such brew is very high on the Lord's list of concerns. But maybe the young fella got a good mark for sincerity.

One man probably wished his devout wife, who could get all teary-eyed in church, would have gotten the inner and outer harnessed up. He didn't care much about going to church with her. He said sadly, "On the way home, she always gives me the devil about something." She needed a "heart attack" of God's love.

Better to be like the story of the little newsboy who sold a paper to a man in a barber shop. Being given a five-dollar bill, he ran out. Onlookers thought he had skipped with the money. Presently, he returned and handed the man his change. When he was told of the accusation, tears came to his eyes. He said, "Mister, I couldn't do that; I'm a Christian." Hooray for authentic Christianity!

"Man looks on the outward appearance but God looks on the heart" (1 Samuel 16:7). Both views ought to look a whole lot alike.

SECTION 4

Creature Tales

Possums and Men

"Grinning like a possum" is one of those sayings you sort of take for granted but don't scrutinize for accuracy. If he grins, he most likely is unaware of his pleasant expression. I can't say I've ever noticed one doing it. I did see one that had about as much to grin about as a kangaroo with a split pouch.

Pretending to be dead is another trait Mr. Possum has down pat. If he's playing dead and escapes harm, he probably grins to himself. The one in this possum tale may have done so many a time, only to rise again. But judging from his appearance on the street, he had as much chance of rising and grinning as the vehicle that clobbered him had of saying "I'm sorry." I mean he was flat-dead, dead.

Now the "passing of the possum" gave rise to a question to ponder: How come he got himself run over? I reckon it wasn't his intention. About the best philosophical answer I could conjure up was this: he got it because he was where he had no business being.

Being where you belong is plain good sense. Like a possum and the woods are as compatible as a hollow log and a squirrel. But he has as much business on a busy city street as a toad frog in a churn of cream. This one would've looked better and lasted longer if he had roamed in his rightful place.

Man may have a drop or two of possum blood in his veins. He's been known to get himself in a mess by getting out of his intended place. May even grin about it. If he does, he looks pretty silly.

Adam and Eve shinnied up the wrong tree. Got driven out of the Garden of Eden. The Lord said, "Cursed is the ground for thy sake: in sorrow shalt thou eat of it all the days of thy life: thorns also and thistles shall it bring forth to thee" (Genesis 3:17-18). Sure wish those folks had behaved. Those "thorns and thistles" of sin have stuck us all.

Peter longed to stay near Jesus. Instead, he warmed at the fire of the Lord's enemies. Accused of being a disciple, "he began to curse and to swear, saying, I know not the man" (Matthew 26:74). Being out of place turned him into a profaner and liar. Not uncommon - then or now. To his credit, he repented, cried a spell, got back in place, and turned out to be a mighty preacher.

Being where we belong is a sight better than being an out-of-place "possum" that's not just playing possum.

Chasing Trucks

A feisty dog running after a ten ton-truck. Not an uncommon sight, but one that's always ridiculous. Most likely, he's yappin', snappin' at the tires, and doing his dogged best to catch the thing.

When one of those "dog-chases-truck" events goes by, a question climbs up in the cab of your mind. What would he do with it, if he caught it? He'd have something on his paws he couldn't handle that could hurt him.

Having it, he'd find he really didn't want it after all. Would've been better off without it. He might decide he'd been had instead of having.

Man has been known to cut up like a canine. He's all the time running after things he's got no business having. If he gets a hold of something God has put His "Thou shalt not" on, he may wish he had shalt notted.

Now God said, "Thou shalt not covet thy neighbor's wife" (Exodus 20:17). In Bible language, it's known as covet-lustness. What's "next door" looks better than what's at home. Like the dog and the truck, the chase is on. God's good laws are run over, a few lives are smashed to smithereens; but he gets what he thought he wanted. More often than not, the "rig" is rigged with trouble. He may take her "for better, for worse," and find out she's worse than he took her for. (The feeling may be mutual.) He ends up with a puzzled look on his face, like a dog with a tire in his mouth. Guilt does that to folks.

Then again, a man may spend a lifetime running after things. Comes home at night with his tongue hanging out, panting. Truck-loads of stuff whet his appetite like Alpo making a dog's mouth water. He just might get overrun with his accumulations. Then he's loaded and run over with care, worry, fear of loss, and worst of all, selfishness. Finds out that being stuffed with stuff leaves a man empty.

Jesus warns, "A man's life consisteth not in the abundance of the things which he possesseth" (Luke 12:15). Ecclesiastes 5:12 says, "The abundance of the rich will not suffer [let] him to sleep."

One man raised such a bumper crop he aimed to build bigger barns to hold it all. He forgot to lay up some treasure in heaven and got labeled "Fool" (Luke 12:16-21).

Before we start chasing "trucks," we'd better check 'em out. They could be loaded.

Mice and Dragons

The way folks sometimes react can be downright funny. Ned Mathews told of an event that had an unexpected summary.

Two ladies went to their vacation home in the mountains. Upon entering, they discovered things on the floor that were usually on shelves. Thinking for sure someone had broken in, they explored cautiously. The culprit was a snake, that, like Santa Claus, had come down the chimney. Couldn't blame him for taking up residence in a nice home, but his presence wasn't the enjoyable kind. Sort of shook the ladies up.

A nearby neighbor was pressed into the snake extractin' business. Soon, nothing of the slithering critter remained but a bad memory. The damsels stood rescued.

Now you'd think finding a snake in the house would unnerve women-folk something awful. And it did. But in this case, things could have been worse. One of the ladies relieved comment indicated such: "It could've been a mouse!"

The Bible says God gives His angels charge over us to protect us. Even says, "Thou shalt tread upon the lion and adder....and the dragon shalt thou trample under feet" (Psalm 91:13). With that kind of guarding, the ladies could face the big spookies, but a mouse would've put the quivers on them. Most likely the angels really did get a "charge" over that.

Maybe we need to be more scared of the destructive little things than we are. We tend to overlook what they can do. We face more "mice" than "dragons," but mice know how to multiply better than a mathematician. First thing you know, they're all over the place. A man's life can become a mice nest.

The Bible warns us to be particular of what's inside us. Hate is equated with murder, lust with adultery, covetousness with stealing, and failing to love with death. The thought may be mouse-size compared to the act, and most of us wouldn't dare do the dastardly deeds. Who, though, has exterminated all the "mice" thoughts that scurry around in the heart? "Mice" can become "dragons."

The little lie can lead to big trouble. The little fuss can eventually destroy a home. A little greed may make a fellow grabby. A touch of bitterness has power to shrivel our souls. A little unbelief can harden our hearts against the Savior. A little inner filth can begin to make a slum of a man's insides.

Paul said, "A little leaven leaveneth the whole lump. Purge out therefore the old leaven, that ye may be a new lump" (1 Corinthians 5:6-7).

Snakes are scary, but if there's a mouse in the house, get him out!

Gorillas and Lambs

A little girl's version of how God made woman goes like this: "When God made man, He looked at him and said, 'I can do better than that. So He made woman.'" That's not exactly Scriptural, but man and woman were something special. They got off to a good start, but sin entered and their natures changed.

When Adam first looked at Eve, he said, "This is now bone of my bones" (Genesis 2:23). It wasn't until after the devil got in his licks that she became a bone of contention. And Adam wasn't far behind. That wasn't God's original intent when He placed them in the Garden of Eden. He meant for them to be happy, but sin has a way of messing things up.

Man's fallen nature can be illustrated by a thing I saw being hawked at the State Fair. The sign said, "Come see a beautiful woman change into a 450-pound gorilla before your eyes." (One young fellow later remarked, "I've seen that happen." And he wasn't talking about a side show, either.) The claim was about as real as a three-dollar-bill, but a similar thing does happen inside of people.

Some men and women in the Bible must've had gorilla-like natures. Ol' evil King Ahab picked a real doozie named Jezebel for a wife. She gave him a fit. Wouldn't be surprised if he later wished she was in a cage instead of on the throne with him.

Herodias acted like a mad gorilla because John the Baptist said she was living in sin as Herod's wife (Mark

6:17-28). She lost her head in anger and John really lost his!

King Solomon is reputed to have been exceptionally wise. And he was. But having seven hundred wives makes you think he sort of blew it in domestic affairs. Some things he wrote about women indicate he tangled with a few whose natures weren't so gentle. He said, "A continual dropping in a very rainy day and a contentious woman are alike" (Proverbs 27:15). Also, "It is better to dwell in a corner of the house top, than with a brawling woman in a wide house" (Proverbs 21:9). Wouldn't be surprised if King Sol didn't scratch his head many a time when it didn't itch.

Undoubtedly, men have the same gorilla-like capacity as the side-show lady. Fact is, many a woman who was as gentle as a lamb to begin with has been transformed into a gorilla by some aggravating man. It works both ways.

The point of this hairy story is that "gorillas"—of both genders—can be turned into "lambs." Jesus is called "the Lamb of God, which taketh away the sin of the world" (John 1:29). When Jesus comes in, the gorilla in us goes out.

There's no "gorilla" too big for Jesus not to make a "lamb" out of him.

Now wouldn't that rattle your cage!

A Greedy Tale

It was a thought-provoking sight. A fat bird, of which species I do not know, perched on the bird feeder's porch. He wasn't eating; just quietly sitting there. Perhaps his craw was full, or maybe he was tired and wanted to rest a while.

Whatever Mr. Bird's roosting reason was, a thought winged its way around in my head. I have no desire to impugn his motive and perhaps be judged "bird brain" by him. But his actions reminded me of traits found in us two-legged, non-flying birds.

Evidently he had had plenty to eat and had staked out the territory as his own. Since he was bigger than the average bird, others were not likely to challenge him. With one flick of his wing, he could have knocked a lesser bird winding.

Now there was enough food for several birds of a feather to flock together, but not a single one tried to "table down" as long as fatso was there. He had more than enough, but somehow he looked rather lonely. I didn't know which to pity more, him or the hungry ones he shut out.

I reckon it was in this particular bird's nature to be a greedy bully, but it seems to me that God created man to fly higher than that.

Man can get his craw full of greed. (Covetousness is a synonym.) The dictionary defines it as "wanting to get more than one's share" or "desiring things that belong to others." One of the Ten Commandments says,

"Don't do that." The root of the problem originates in the heart (Mark 7:21-22).

Greed says "what's mine is mine and you'll not have it. Furthermore, what's yours is mine, and I'll have it if I can get it."

A greedy-hearted person often victimizes the helpless, leaving misery and brokeness in its wake. But the victimizer always robs his own soul. It sort of shrivels up. Too, greed in the heart, but not acted on, is greed still, causing soul damage.

Jesus paints a picture of greed in the story of the man who was robbed on the Jericho Road. The thieves "stripped him of his clothes, beat him and went away, leaving him half dead" (Luke 10:30 NIV). Without realizing it, the robbers robbed themselves, too. It works that way. That "Jericho Road" runs around the world and through every generation.

I don't suppose the main character in this bird-tale will ever change into a benevolent creature. He will be a fowl with a few foul ways as long as he wings his way from place to place. But man has the capacity for higher flying. Through Jesus, he can soar on new wings that lift him above the polluted atmosphere of greed and grasping.

Jesus provides a "feeder," laden with food for the soul: "Thou shalt love thy neighbor as thyself." Perch there and feast. Greed will die of malnutrition.

Parable of the Yelping Pups

Six-thirty in the morning is not the best time to awaken to the frantic sounds of thirteen pups. But it happened.

We were visiting our son, Mark, and his wife, Debbie, in Georgia. On a beautiful piece of rolling land, their living quarters are atop a barn which is home for six horses, two dogs and, for awhile, thirteen pups.

Bo and Bell's six-week-old golden retriever children occupied one of the stalls. On the morning in question, the combined chorus of pitiful cries sounded like a snake or some varmint was about to devour the helpless pups.

The heroic urge hit, so down to the rescue I went. Mark was already there, looking and listening to the shrill yapping of the little ones. After I inquired as to the cause of the disturbance, Mark said, "They're just hungry." I didn't know anything that hungry could yell like that for some breakfast.

Now the pups were as helpless as six-week-old babies. Ma Bell waited outside the stall, ready to serve breakfast. But Mark had to open the heavy door. She stood kind of spread-eagle like, bracing herself for the attack.

As Grandpa McCoy would say, "She could only set places for ten," but there were thirteen mouths to feed. You never heard such smacking and slurping, with three at a time rooting and pushing for a place at the table.

As each one got its fill, it would walk away. Finally, about three were still loading up, and ol' Bell was in a sitting position, leaning against a stall door. She looked plumb tuckered and seemed right anxious for the younguns to go play.

With their stomachs as tight as a kettle drum, the pups were soon fast asleep. No more yelping, no more disturbing the peace. Mark had served them the milk of human kindness in opening the door, but Ma Bell had served them the milk of Mama's love. It took both to satisfy the need.

A drama of life unfolded. There's a lot of hunger in the world—the heart kind and the physical kind. Being locked in circumstances, some can't open the door for themselves. But they cry. Until some "Mark" comes along, need and supply are kept apart. When they are joined, hunger is relieved.

The Bible tells of the hungry multitude needing to be fed. There was food available with Jesus, but He told His disciples, "Give ye them to eat" (Matthew 14:15-20). They had the privilege of distribution. Through them, supply met need.

Christians are to be door openers to bring the hungry to Jesus, the Bread of Life. And through us, He can provide food for the body and food for the soul.

The world would be a lot quieter if folks and Jesus could get together.

A Frog with a Tale

For a toad frog he was about as cute as such a critter is expected to be. He would fit in the palm of a hand, if such a wart-risking hand desired that kind of company.

But Toady was where he ought not to be: on the screened-in back porch.

Not being into frog gigging, and having no intention of doing bodily harm to the little fella, I propped the door open and shooed him out. His exit turned out to be temporary.

A day or two later, there he was again. The sneaky little cuss had hopped in when someone opened the door. He wasn't any more welcome than before. The shooing out process was repeated.

Now Toady has to be given credit for persistence. He had an unusual attraction for the porch. It seemed to lure him like magnet does metal. He managed to put his hopper in gear and get in again. Once he was spotted waiting for the door to open so he could pay a call. Being encouraged to take his presence elsewhere, he headed toward the woods.

At this writing, he has been looked for, expected, but not seen. Wishing him no misfortune, I hope he has been to toad school, learning that porches are not equipped with lily pads, and nourishment is scarce. Besides that, a less friendly homeowner just might stomp the living daylights out of him.

Toad talk is not a common language, but if communication were possible, someone should tell Toady the truth. He was lucky to trespass forbidden territory on the porch so many times, yet be treated with compassion. Even got the chance to fulfill his froggy destiny by returning to the woods.

A drop or two of toad blood must run in human veins. Man is all the time hopping into places where he shouldn't.

Jesus told about a young fella lured by wine, women, and song. Ended up singing the blues in a hogpen. His daddy's love bridged the miles, and his smelly boy headed home. Instead of receiving a verbal clobbering, he was received with compassion. Got himself restored and headed in the right direction (Luke 15:11-24).

And that's the truth of the compassionate love of God, demonstrated through Christ and the cross. Don't play leapfrog with that liberating, life-changing truth.

SECTION 5

On Being A Child

Essay of Childishness

Childishness is a right common malady. There's a difference in being childlike and being childish. Jesus commends childlikeness— humble, teachable, trusting, loving.

Childishness includes wanting our own way, temper tantrums, sulking, refusing to play fairly, a "me-first" attitude.

Blindness to self makes distinguishing between the two tricky. It's about as hard to step outside ourselves for a scrutinizing look as it is to see clearly in a broken mirror.

A man complained of how childish and immature his wife was. Said she was just like a kid, fussing, throwing tantrums. He said, "I was taking a bath. She came in, and, for no reason, began hollering. Pitched a real fit. Then she sank my little boats and threw my rubber ducky out of the bathtub!"

Imbedded in each of us is a little kid. He's hard to spot but jumps out of hiding at unexpected times. Too often, we invite the youngun out to play. He's eager and ready.

Paul said, "When I was a child, I spoke, understood, and thought as a child." In the vernacular, he was saying he was a normal kid. Then he added, "But when I became a man, I put away childish things." (That doesn't mean putting our kid's toys away.) It means he grew up and stopped acting childish.

Immature attitudes crop up in churches all too often.

Not a few members start out in the Beginner Department, never to get any higher than the "Aginner" Department. These are the folks who are "agin" everything the church tries to do. Unless it's their pet project. Hinders progress considerably.

A choir member, who was no Sandi Patty, insisted on making melody from the front row. Got mad when asked to render from the second row. Praise to the Lord was lost in the shuffle.

A deacon, who loved to pray in public, felt slighted when he wasn't called on to beseech the Lord as often as he thought he should be. He sulked by keeping score on a calendar and used it against the pastor. That must've impressed the Lord greatly.

A "Soldier of the Cross" gets crossed up over some church matter and deserts the Lord's army. Won't even join another unit. My, how the Lord must grieve.

The Bible says we should "be no more children," but should "grow up into Him [Christ] in all things" (Ephesians 4:14-15).

Going from rompers to grown-up takes a while. Rompered adult Christians need a good application of spiritual Vigero.

Now, if you will excuse me, I'll go draw my bath water. Would someone please hand me my little sailboats and my rubber ducky?

Table Talk

Seminary students, fortunate enough to be called to serve churches, are enriched. That usually doesn't mean fat bank accounts but rich in memorable experiences. Traveling to church fields on weekends involves staying in numerous homes and eating at tables not a few.

Our next-door seminary friends had such a weekend arrangement with their church. Their little son, Bruce, would go with them. On one occasion they wished he hadn't.

Children can be embarrassingly honest, making parents as red-faced as a ripe tomato. Everybody had tabled down for a fine, Sunday country meal. The table was heavily laden with all kinds of goodies. The nice lady said, "Bruce, do you want some beans and potatoes?" Expecting a polite "Yes, ma'am," his answer must've been more like being hit in the face with a wet dishrag. He said, "Naw; I want somethin' better'n that."

No doubt they all laughed, but the reverend and his helpmate most likely found themselves sitting on the edge of their chairs. Wouldn't be surprised if they wished they had stuffed a biscuit in his mouth before he could answer.

A bit of truth can be dished up and served from the question and answer. Compared to what God offers us, the fare of this world is "beans and potatoes." Now folks can exist on such but, spiritually speaking, God's table is loaded with "pheasant-under-glass." And He says, "No good thing will He withhold from them that walk uprightly" (Psalm 84:11). The "upright" can sit "downright" for a real feast.

Now "Ol' Scratch" can cook up some real aromatic dishes. You might say he makes them from scratch. He has culinary skills that set taste buds to tingling. It's best, though, to remember where his kitchen is. What he serves has the fire of hell in it and is apt to burn whoever eats his dainties.

He offers "the pleasures of sin," but omits to say they are "for a season" (Hebrews 11:25). He sets a mighty attractive table, but his grub is peppered with destruction.

Jesus invites us to partake from His table. What He serves will satisfy and never give spiritual indigestion.

"Ye cannot be partakers of the Lord's table, and the tables of devils" (1 Corinthians 10:21).

When the devil says, "Have something from my table," learn to say, "Naw; I want somethin' better'n that!"

Bubbles

It was one of those unforgettable moments that etches itself on an onlooker's mind, surfacing occasionally as a lovely memory.

Seventeen-month-old grandson, Taylor, and his pretty mama, Debbie, like to play. She's never too busy or too tired to have a good time with the littlest angel in the family.

Once upon a time, out on the second story-deck, under the Georgia sun, the game was bubble making. Mama would dip the plastic ring in the jar of soapy stuff and swing it in the air. A whole covey of beautiful bubbles would fly in all directions. Big bubbles, little ones, round ones, oblong ones. Tinted with rainbow colors, they would float downward to the deck, as gravity did its gentle work.

Taylor, with store-bought toys galore, was bubbling with joy over the fragile, inexpensive little spheres that were weaving and bobbing and dancing on air all around him. What a delight to see him, with a little blue straw hat askew on his curly head, gleeful sounds coming from a laughing face, punching bubbles with a pointing finger or stomping one with a prancing foot.

Mama's laughter and pride in the little fellow's bubble bursting talent added to the event like icing on a cake. Papa's heart reveled at the sight of pure joy and boundless love.

The scene was something of a parable of life. The Bible poses a question philosophers have grappled with for centuries: "For what is your life?" Then a simply profound answer follows. "It is even a vapor, that appeareth for a little time, then vanisheth away" (James 4:14). In light of eternity, one's earthly life is fragile and brief. Like a bubble.

Yet within that allotted span of time, things appear that may last but a little while, bringing joy and creating memories. Like watching a sunset at the beach as the great ball of fire seems to be extinguished in the ocean. Or hearing a hauntingly beautiful song that vibrates in the heart from then on.

It may be watching cumulus clouds forming funny faces in the sky. Or whiffing the fragrance of a rambling rose. Maybe it's seeing a happy child riding on the merry-go-round at the fair.

Then there are deeper moments. Like hearing someone say for the first time, "I love you." Or that initial experience of inviting Jesus to come live in your heart, and it becomes a permanent relationship. Or a time when God answers a prayer just like you wanted Him to.

Jesus said we must become like little children to enter God's Kingdom. Maybe that means, in part, that we have to have childlike eyes and hearts like little Taylor to see the beautiful bubbles that come within our reach. To see them before they burst and disappear.

Love's Motivation

Most of us need a little motivation to shift us into high gear. Sometimes it comes from a least-expected source.

Granddaughter Valerie was about five. The little Georgia belle came for a visit and found her Papa sick abed. The punies had jumped all over him, making living somewhat of a chore.

She did her best to bring sunshine into the room with her little-girl chatter, smiles, and honest-to-goodness sympathy. It worked, too, making Papa's day considerably brighter. But it was her parting words that made her visit so unforgettable. From the depth of her tender little heart, and with sincere feeling, she said,

"Papa, if you die, I *hope* I can come to your funeral." And out the door she went.

Well now, her uttered concern would put some second thoughts into a person's head. It's like reading the small print at the bottom of an insurance policy. Can be a real shocker.

I'm not sure that I got well immediately, but I made up my mind to do so as pronto as possible. Valerie made me feel it was get up or end up with viewers of the remains saying in hushed tones, "My, doesn't he look natural." The ol' adrenaline began pumping, and I was motivated to think another mountain or two could be climbed.

Underneath the words that added mobility to life was something more valuable than gold. It was pure love, flowing from the guileless heart of a little child. She was saying, "Papa, I love you." It was her somewhat unconventional way of expressing her love—even unto death.

Love is about the most powerful motivator there is. Especially God's love. It will get a person going when everything else fails. To know that somebody cares makes the heart beat a little faster and the soul reach a little higher.

Jesus was all the time lifting people up. He's the world class, premiere motivator. Like the time He had a nighttime chat with a man named Nicodemus. Brother Nic was in the dark about a theological question. Lovingly, Jesus lifted him into the light of truth.

In the course of their conversation, Jesus told about God's love for the entire world. He said something that has moved and lifted countless numbers of folks right into heaven itself. "For God so loved the world, that He gave His only begotten Son, that whosoever believes in Him should not perish, but have everlasting life" (John 3:16). Glory be!

That's motivational love. Makes a person want to crawl out of the bed of soulsickness and start living a wholesome life. To believe in Jesus is to experience His elevating love.

The old hymn tune has it right: "When nothing else could help, *love lifted me!*" Yes-sirree-bob.

To Tell the Truth

Little children can be as straightforward as a bowman's arrow. They tend to tell things as they see, hear, or feel them, with a strong measure of innocence. It has to do with openheartedness and truthfulness.

This was illustrated in a story Pastor Jim Potts shared. One day his little boy answered the phone. After hanging up, his mother wanted to know who it was. He said, "It was some woman who wanted to know if Mr. Potts would marry a divorced woman." "And what did you tell her?" inquired inquisitive Mom. "I told her I don't think so; he's married to my mama," replied the guileless little one. Now that's transparent openness.

Then again, hard-rock truth-telling can be tomato-red embarrassing. Like the story of a woman who saw unexpected company approaching. She said, "I'd just as soon see the devil coming as to see that woman." Opening the door, the unwanted visitor was greeted with a toothy smile and words as warm as the summer sun of how glad she was to see her.

One thing the less-than-honest host hadn't counted on: her little girl with fine-tuned hearing and an uninhibited mouth. Mamma's gushiness called for correction. "But Mama, you just said you'd just as soon see the devil coming." Not much chance of a repeat visit after that burst of truthfulness.

Then there are times when church can be the setting for unexpected, no-guile utterances.

The preacher had concluded his mighty, soul-stirring sermon. The invitation for broken-hearted sinners to come to the front had been issued. On the invitation hymn, a little boy made his way toward the outstretched hand of the pleased parson. Undoubtedly the responder was moved, but his question must've startled the preacher. "Where's the bathroom?" was the urgent request. Wouldn't be surprised if the watchful angels didn't smile at that one.

The little guy probably never realized he had done something out of the ordinary and the preacher wasn't about to tell. Chalk one up for open-hearted truthfulness.

Jesus said we have to become as little children to enter the Kingdom of Heaven. Maybe that includes having a heart as open toward Him as all outdoors and being as truthful as two-plus-two equals four.

No wonder He set a little child in the midst of the people to show them what they must become like in order to become a part of God's family.

Seeing from a New Perspective

Hoke, in the movie, "Driving Miss Daisy," made a deep, insightful statement. Having been her chauffeur for years, Hoke found that his eyesight had dimmed a little. He had offered to drive her to some desired destination, but she said, "Hoke, you're too old, and besides, you can't see." His respectful response was, "Miss Daisy, how you know how I see lessen you see with my eyes?"

That's the equivalent of having to walk in the other person's shoes to understand his lot in life.

Most of us are Olympic-grade broad jumpers when it comes to jumping at conclusions. We are apt to judge a person's actions, words, or thoughts, without a hint of where he's coming from. Our backgrounds have a lot to do with what we are.

Unless we see with the other person's eyes or walk in his shoes, our judgments can be about as correct as a third grader trying his hand at calculus.

Mark, observing little children giving parents a hard time, said a kid of his would never act that way. That was before he had a "kid."

A few years later, his lovable three-and-a-half-year-old son pitched right much of a fit in a store. Got down on the floor and did some hollering. In public, mind you. That evening, Mark was going to get to the bottom of things.

Having seen the "make eye-contact, question and answer technique" by a child psychologist on TV, he said, "Taylor, why did you act so ugly today?"

With a little face twisting, as in deep thought, Taylor said slowly, "Well, I ate a banana, and the seeds in the banana made me do it." So much for child psychology. Laughter erupted, probably saving Taylor's bottom.

The point is that Mark can now identify with other parents whose children jump the traces at times. Funny thing, though, he's graveyard-silent about what his child would never do.

Crow is tough to chew, and hard to swallow, sometimes getting hung in the esophagus. But it can be right nourishing and puts you in touch with humanity.

One of the many things we love about Jesus is that He became one of us—but without sin. "And the Word [Christ] was made flesh, and dwelt among us" (John 1:14). He knows what we face, having walked in our shoes. He sees with our eyes.

He even loves us when, occasionally, we get down on the floor for a spell of kicking and screaming. He doesn't condone it, neither does He condemn us. He knows it's not banana seeds that cause our ugliness, but our sinful nature. For that, He went to the cross to deliver us.

Because Jesus identifies with us, we can "come boldly unto the throne of grace, that we may obtain mercy, and find grace to help in time of need" (Hebrews 4:16).

"Lord, how do you know how I see?" His reply: "I've been there."

A Boy and His Horse

Annie Lind was three-year-old Taylor's "best friend." She was a horse. A horse with a sad history. At age thirteen, she was laced with drugs by her shady horse trader owner to hide the painful problem in her front legs and hooves and sold at auction.

It didn't take but about three days for her new owners to find out an endurance mount she wasn't. Trail riding was out.

For seven years she was a pet, treated with kindness and even surgery to try to ease her pain, but among horses there is a pecking order. Annie's age and illness placed her at the bottom. She was an outcast among the other horses and was frequently kicked or bitten. Mark, Taylor's dad, knew that someday she would have to be "put down," but dreaded the doing of it.

One Sunday morning, Honey, the number-three horse, cornered Annie Lind in the shelter and nearly kicked the life out of her. The vet agreed that "her time had come." She was put to sleep and buried in a backhoe-dug big hole out in the pasture.

Now little Taylor could ride this gentle horse and loved to lead her around by her halter. He had planned to do so on that fateful Sunday afternoon. When told that Annie had died, he was mighty upset. They showed him where she was buried, but at three, death is a mystery that's hard to understand. All he knew was his horse was buried in that big hole.

Later that day, I saw Taylor sitting in the recliner, head bowed and resting on his supporting hand. My heart was aching for him. I asked, "Are you sad?" He said, "Yes." "What are you sad about?" "That mean man buried my favorite horse, and it hurt my feelings." I felt like crying.

I tried to explain about dying and burying, without much success. To him, she was still alive, and he planned to go out and "un-dig her and she would be all right." His Aunt Hannah gave a try at consolation by fancifully telling him that Annie Lind had gone to heaven. He said, "I'm going up there and close the clouds and bring her back down here."

A mixture of emotions was triggered inside the little fella: anger, sadness, hurt feelings, loneliness, broken heart, helplessness, a longing to see his "best friend" again, a need to be loved, and a reluctance to accept death.

Annie Lind's sad life and Taylor's sadness somehow meshed. Two weeks afterwards, he said, "A long time ago I had a horse named Annie Lind." I reckon she will always live in the tender spot in his heart where memories are kept. Otherwise she would be just a name carved on a stall door in the barn.

Folks of all ages are acquainted with the same range of emotions when some person whom we love dies. It's part of being human.

But there's God's available strengthening gift—FAITH IN JESUS CHRIST! His gracious words have comforted many a heart. "I am the resurrection, and the life: he that believeth in me, though he were dead, yet shall he live," said death's Conqueror (John 11:25).

That great promise calms our own runaway emotions and the hurting heart finds peace.

Sawdust and Planks

Children are great teachers. Sometimes they help grownups to see themselves in a true light.

Grandson Taylor, about three, was on a trail ride with his mama and daddy. It was Mark's turn to ride. At the campsite, Debbie was keeping Taylor in the living quarters of the horse trailer.

Apparently, it wasn't one of Taylor's better days. His determination and Debbie's mothering had created a mild civil war. When Mark came in, exasperated Mama was giving him a report on the little rebel's resistance to authority.

Now Taylor, seated on the bed, was listening to his conduct report and must've felt a need for self-defense. Somewhere along the line he had been told "shut up" was not acceptable as part of his vocabulary.

In the midst of the somewhat tense atmosphere, the little fellow injected some damaging evidence into the trial. With an accusing finger, pointing in his "prosecutor's" direction, he convincingly said, "I believe SHE said 'shut up.' She did. She said, 'shut up.'" Bingo! Double exposure.

Case dismissed. Tension flew out the window, laughter replaced frustration, and a truce was reached.

Debbie is as fine a little mama as you can find. Wouldn't be surprised, though, if she didn't have to admit she was out-maneuvered by her wary offspring.

Maybe this trail-ride episode can put us on the trail of a question Jesus asked a long time ago. He knew that folks have twenty-twenty vision when viewing the faults of others and are blind as a bat to their own.

"Why do you look at the speck of sawdust in your brother's eye and pay no attention to the plank in your own eye?" said the One who came to help us to see ourselves (Matthew 7:3, NIV).

In plain words, He's telling us to do something about our own imperfections before we magnify those in others. There may be some "sawdust" in a brothers eye, but ol' "plankeye" is not the one to remove it. Plank-extracting must come first. Then we can see clearly to apply some "eyewash" to the other fella.

Even Can be Uneven

Revenge. Who of us doesn't know the sudden surge of "eye for eye, tooth for tooth"? Even in Christians, the old fallen nature is still kicking around inside, demanding his way. If he's not kept in a straight jacket, he's likely to get loose. He'll take a whack at whoever laid a hurting on us. Sometimes with our approval. It's called getting even.

The desire to get even is born in us. Shows itself early. When our grandson, Daniel, was about three years old, he got up a head of steam at his older brother, Mark. What Mark did is unknown, but Daniel had probable cause against him. Now the little one lisped on some words, but he was spunky, not letting the lack of clarity of speech stop him. So he balled up his little fist and showed it to Mark, saying, "Mark, ya thee thith?" I don't know whether he let him have it or not, but he sure wanted to. Shows a three-year-old is not exactly unacquainted with revengeful leanings. That's not too hard to understand—in a child.

The problem gets more serious in bigger kids. A teenager strutted around with tough words emblazoned on his shirt: "I don't get mad—I get even." He may have thought he was the cock-of-the-walk, but there's always a bigger rooster around that's bent on revenge, too. Makes for trouble.

Even the great King David had his moments when he didn't feel too kindly toward his enemies. He requested this of God: "As a snail which melteth, let every one of them pass away...and let them make a noise like a dog, and go round about the city" (Psalm 58:8 and Psalm 59:14). If we can lay aside our piosity for a second or two, we can admit that we know the feeling. That's not to say it's right; just that it's there.

A better way is in Jesus who said, "Love your enemies, bless them that curse you, do good to them that hate you, and pray for them which despitefully use you" (Matthew 5:44). Now that's not only hard, it's impossible - if we try it alone. We have to let Jesus do it through us. We bless 'em out; He blesses. He never shares our desire for revenge.

Mr. brother-in-law, Art Fore, tells of his pastor who was a victim of a cantankerous church member. A real fault finder. Repeatedly the pastor said to his wife, "I'm going to get even with that man." Puzzled her. One day he came home and said, "Well, I got even. Brother So-and-So needed a blood transfusion, and I gave him my blood." They got on even terms and became friends. Sound like Jesus?

The Bible says, "Vengeance is mine; I will repay, saith the Lord" (Romans 12:19). God knows how to do it. We don't. He tells us to feed and water the enemy and leave score keeping to Him. Sometimes we're tempted to try to save the Lord the trouble. But He might say, "I'd rather do it Myself." We'd better let Him.

Christmas Memories

Christmas of '88 came on Sunday. An appropriate time to celebrate the birth of Him who caused Christmas to be. Grownups understand that; children may have a problem with it. Going to church on Christmas Day tends to dethrone St. Nick whose wares are more appealing than hymn singing and sermonizing.

When the mind is at home and the body is in church, a cross-pull takes over. That's what happened.

The letters C H R I S T were used, hopefully with appropriate comments about each letter. Counting an introduction, five points, a conclusion and a prayer, it wasn't exactly a sermonette or "a little talk." It was a full sermon.

On the way home, a just barely teenager, discussing the sermon, expressed relief to his mother. "I sure am glad his name wasn't Nebuchadnezzer." Right on, young fella. Me, too!

Christmas is a good time to build memories. Good ones last a lifetime. Some Yuletide songs suggest things

I've never done. Like "chestnuts roasting by an open fire." Fact is, I don't remember eating chestnuts, ever. Or "Bring us some figgy pudding." Sounds kinda, well, figgy. "Dreaming of a white Christmas" is more to my liking, to which I plead guilty of having done.

Moving pictures of Christmases past project on the mind's screen.

Buying Christmas trees that looked like they needed me became an annual joke. They looked a little forlorn, but the price was right. The artificial one now used is right pretty, but I miss the ribbings of yesteryears.

Hanging stockings for Santa to stuff, putting out cookies for his snack, telling giggling children to hush and go to sleep constituted part of the night before Christmas.

On Christmas morning, four wide-eyed children would line up by age to see what the jolly old elf had left. "Ho, Ho, Ho" and "Merry Christmas" were the soundtrack to which they marched, the joy on their faces making all the preparations worthwhile.

Jesus, the Star of Bethlehem, is the Star of Christmas, so every year, Harriett bakes a birthday cake for Jesus. In the afternoon, the family gathers for a carol sing, reading the Christmas story from the Bible, and talking with Jesus in prayer. Then the candle on the cake is lit, and "Happy Birthday, dear Jesus" peals out from our hearts in joyful song. It becomes the highlight of the day. His promise of "where two or three are gathered together in My Name, there am I in the midst of them" (Matthew 18:20) is fulfilled.

The listening heart hears the angel saying, "Unto you is born this day in the city of David a Savior, which is Christ the Lord" (Luke 2:11). And that's when we hear the "Bells on Christmas Day" ringing clear and true. What if the whole world could hear them?

More Than Cheese

Without being fed, both body and soul get skinny. Their hunger must be satisfied.

Four-year-old Taylor was told if he didn't eat at suppertime, he would go to bed without any snacks.

Children have a way of pushing parents to the limit, testing to see if their words are real or just empty threats. Taylor pushed.

Finding himself in a nice bed didn't satisfy the hungries gnawing at his empty stomach. Presently, his request for something to eat was met with a firm "no." Even repeating the earlier admonition that no supper-eating meant no eating until breakfast didn't quiet him for long.

As Daddy and Mama sat in the living room, with full stomachs, a plaintive voice came from the bedroom: "Hey, you guys, would you let a fella have a little piece of cheese?" Now, what well-stuffed parent could deny such a cry of impending starvation?

There was no request for cookies, just something basic to ward off perishing in the night. Amidst laughter and pity, the intended lesson and punishment would have to wait. "Just a little piece of cheese," and probably a little something else, to the rescue! Maybe even a hug for the wary little guy.

While slaves in Egypt, ancient Israel fared pretty well on a basic diet. Then, on their march to freedom, God sent them manna. He said it was "bread from heaven" (Exodus 16:4). To us folks, 3500 years removed, that sounds like an improvement over that to which they were accustomed. Something like going from fatback to T-bone steak. But they got tired of the manna and longed for the food of the "good old days" of slavery.

Many a misguided person is suffering from malnutrition of the soul. Not knowing what all of that inner growling is all about, he tries to satisfy soul-hunger with the so-called food of this world. He may try fame, fortune, or whatever tastes good for a while but finds they are about as soul-filling as cotton candy at the State Fair.

Then, some "darkness of night" eclipses his life. Finding himself filled with emptiness, he cries out, "Lord, would You let me have 'a little piece of cheese?'"

But God is gracious. He nourishes the hungry heart with Jesus, who said, "I am the bread of life: [the bread which came down from heaven]: he that cometh to Me shall never hunger" (John 6:35, 41). Manna from above!

As the soul feasts on Jesus, the hunger pains subside. No need to be skinny-souled children of God. He wants us to be well-nourished on the inside.

The devil puts us to bed as spiritually empty and miserable as he is. The Lord enables us to sing, "I am satisfied with Jesus." Our hearts become as a land "flowing with milk and honey," for He fills our emptiness with Himself. "A little piece of cheese?" No. It's more like a picnic basket from heaven.

And He serves His nourishing food on a platter of love.

Lessons from the Lips of a Little Lad

Jesus spoke of big folks having to be more like little folks to enter the Kingdom. Taking a little child in His arms, He emphasized the necessity of humility. That admirable trait can be the parent of guileless openness.

Four-year-old grandson David must be a descendant of Nathanael in whom Jesus said there was not deceit.

The folding tray, upon which he sometimes eats in the living room, was broken. "I don't know how it happened," said puzzled Dad.

David was standing within earshot of the remark. Without hesitation, he said, "I stood on it." Mystery solved. Honesty and purity of heart shone like the stars above.

One morning David got up pretty late. His mother wondered why he didn't get going at his usual time. She inquired: "David, why did you sleep so long?" His answer seemed reasonable to him: "I was having a good dream, and I woke up. I went back to sleep to finish the dream." He was living in hope.

No doubt many of us got cut off in the middle of some desirable dream but found out that dreams are not like a continued TV series. Maybe a lesson can be learned that even in our waking hours many a good dream is never completed.

The outcome of some things have to be left in the hands of our loving Father. Those are the times we live in hope; for hope is like a golden thread, woven into the fabric of the Christian's life.

Paul assures us, "He who began a good work in you will carry it on to completion until the day of Christ Jesus" (Philippians 1:6, NIV). That kind of hope guarantees a future with promise!

Then there are times when a little one can crawl so deep into our heart that it sings a melodious tune.

Church was over; departure time had come. David and his grandmama were having a conversation out front. At the end of the conversation, he wasn't quite finished.

"Grandmama," he said, "and one more thing: I love you." Turned out to be the icing on the cake.

That's one of those sayings we never tire of hearing. There was some mutual hugging after those reassuring words were spoken, and the ride home had a special glow in it. Though there was a parting of the ways for awhile, they were still joined in heart. Love has a way of doing that. Especially expressed love. More conversations need to end with those heartwarming words: "I love you."

Without knowing it, little David became the lips through which God set forth lessons about honesty, hope, and love. And they came from the sincere heart of a child who already knows that Jesus loves him.

Precious are the words of the Master, "Verily I say unto you, except ye be converted and become as little

children, ye shall not enter the Kingdom of heaven"
(Matthew 18:3).

The world could use some more examples of grown
folks with a childlike heart. Yea, verily.

SECTION 6

Floating Memories

A Handful of Memories

Holding hands with your mother-in-law is not a widespread practice. When it happens, heartstrings are touched.

"Miss" Teeny, Alzheimer's patient, received loving care at the Winston-Salem Baptist Home. One day daughter Harriett was feeding her. One hand lay drawn and immobile, but the other reached out to hold Harriett's, making feeding on the difficult side. So I held her hand, while Harriett patiently coaxed her to eat.

My mind was on that octogenarian's hands, as thoughts began weaving a tapestry with threads of memories. Hands, rather small, slightly gnarled with arthritis, prominently veined, a bit wrinkled, but soft and agedly beautiful.

These were the hands of a faithful wife who wore her wedding rings with honor. Hands that created beauty in the home. Hands that loved to chop in the garden and sweep the yard. Hands gifted in kitchen culinary, preparing tastebud-tickling meals. At family gatherings, she stirred stew in an old iron kettle over an outdoor fire. The grandchildren called her "Markie," so it was "Markie Stew."

These were the hands of a schoolteacher, writing lessons on blackboard or paper. Hands of encouragement to little children trying to learn.

These were willing hands of a daughter, giving loving care to a mother who died at ninety-three, doing all that's involved in meeting the necessary demands of the old, without reluctance.

These were loving hands, extended in greeting family and friends or waving good-bye to the departing. Hands that wrote lengthy letters of interesting chit-chat or words of love and encouragement.

These were the hands that held a hymn book in the church choir and a Bible for spiritual nourishment. Hands folded in prayer. Being Christian hands, guided by the Holy Spirit, she used them to build, not tear down.

"Who shall ascend into the hill of the Lord? Or who shall stand in His holy place?" asks the Psalmist. "He that hath clean hands, and a pure heart," comes the answer. "Miss" Teeny qualifies—past, present, and future. Having put her hands in the nail-scarred hands of Jesus, she will lift them in praise to God throughout eternity.

I felt honored that day to hold a hand that had done so much good all the days of her life. How much better the world would be were there more hands like hers. Gently I let the hand go, but the aroused recollections abide.

She is now on the other shore, among that living host, waving a welcome to others crossing over to God's eternal heaven.

Remembering

"**G**od has given memories that we can have roses in December." What a beautiful thought by James M. Barris. I would like to borrow it.

Long after a pleasant thing has happened, it slumbers in our memory. Any one of our five senses can awaken it, causing us to take a trip down memory lane—with a touch of nostalgia or longing. God knew we needed such a treasure-house in our hearts and graciously provided it.

A few examples may lift the latch on memory's door.

I looked at an old song book. In it are songs of the past that bring a warm glow to older hearts. "Long, Long Ago" is a love song that expresses what many hearts have felt, arousing fond memories.

"Do you remember the path where we met,
Long, long ago, long, long ago?
Ah, yes, you told me you ne'er would forget,
Long, long ago, long ago.
Then, to all others, my smile you preferr'd
Love, when you spoke, gave a charm to each word,
Still my heart treasures the praises I heard,
Long, long ago, long ago."

Silently I hear the tune. Seeing my mother-in-law's name on the cover, I remember singing-sessions around the piano. And I remember happy courtship days with her sweet daughter - not unlike the words of the song.

I look at a stickpin in my tie. Suddenly Dad lives, for he wore it before it was handed down to me years ago. And the good times we shared reach across the span of time.

I look at a thirty-three-year-old floor lamp from seminary days. Every house we've lived in since comes alive. Memories of all descriptions bunch up together and bid for attention. Both tears and laughter mingle.

Jesus left us the Memorial Supper to help us remember. We eat a bit of broken bread and sip the fruit of the vine, hearing His words, "Take, eat; this is My body, which is broken for you: this do in remembrance of Me...This cup is the new covenant in My blood: this do ye, as oft as ye drink it, in remembrance of Me" (1 Corinthians 11:24-25). In so doing, He steps out of the past. He and His cross become unforgettable. And remembering what He has done for us makes us long to see Him. He says we shall!

Could there be some link between those precious memories of the past and the glorious future that awaits us in Christ? Some fulfillment there that's incomplete here? To be sure, to be sure!

"Precious memories, how they linger,
How they ever flood my soul!"

And, thanks be to God, they do.

A Christmas Story

On that first Christmas, the angels brought tidings of great joy. And so it is that the celebration of the birth of the Christ Child is a celebration of joy. But where is Christmas joy when sickness and death are present? Two remembered events answer that question.

Uncle Wilbur was the victim of that relentless, mind-robbing disease, Alzheimer's. Teamed with pneumonia, the final curtain fell. His spirit joined the thirteen other brothers and sisters who, over a span of some eighty years, had preceded him into eternity.

The funeral was not a dirge but a paean. Nieces and nephews formed the choir, singing the songs of the Christian faith. The music he once played on the piano was with us in those moments. The beautifully read Scriptures and appropriate remarks by the pastor dwelt on victory in Jesus. Gradually we were aware of the Presence of the Christ of Christmas. He seemed to say to the listening heart, "Grieve softly; for he is with Me, and I am with you."

On a chilly, sunny December Sunday, Uncle Wilbur's body was laid to rest to await the sound of the trumpet when "the dead in Christ shall rise" (1 Thessalonians 4:16). And all because of Christmas.

The remaining sister is "Miss" Teeny, my mother-in-law. She also suffers from Alzheimer's and is in nursing care. A visit was made, a blessing was to be received.

Her daughter, Harriett, leaning over the bed began singing some of her mother's favorite songs, as her great niece, Peggy, played the electronic keyboard. "Sing, Mother," Harriett would say. And Mother, whose power of recognizing the family has long since gone, by lip reading followed the words with an intermingling of soprano and alto.

"Silent Night," "Away in a Manger," "Life's Railway to Heaven," "Jingle Bells," and "My Jesus, I Love Thee" wafted gently through the room. From the depth of that reverent heart and out of the deep recesses of a once-brilliant mind, came the songs of yesteryear. And we relived those precious days of family gatherings at Christmas time, when we sang together.

It was fitting to read the Christmas story from the Bible in which she had marked special verses in her knowing days. Luke's account made us feel that we were there at that first Christmas. She lay quietly as one awed by the Presence of God. As we joined hands and prayed, she made sounds of earnest agreement.

We did not see Jesus, but suddenly "the glory of the Lord shown round about us," and we knew He was there. Unlike the ancient shepherds, we were not afraid. We were caught up in the love of the Christ of Christmas.

Whether in the darkness of death, the despair of sickness or in times when the sun is shining, Christmas is "Emmanuel— God with us!" (Matthew 1:23).

"Joy to the world: the LORD IS COME!"

Whole Hog or Bologna

The Civil War ended over a hundred years ago. This story is not intended to be another Ft. Sumter and is not a slam on North or South. It's just a funny little yarn spun at a crossroads known as Brinkleyville, North Carolina.

Aunt Edythe was a keen businesswoman with a ready answer for most questions. A northern traveler stopped at her general store. Noticing a jar of peculiar-looking stuff on the counter, he asked a real sensible question: "What in the world is that?" "Pickled pig's feet," came the matter-of-fact reply.

Now it's not the best judgment for a Yankee to try to match wits with a Southern belle in her own territory. This one gave it a try. He said, "You Southerners eat every part there is about a hog, don't you?" That was calculated to be as cute as the curl in a pig's tail. He miscalculated.

As quick as you can say "oink," the unwary traveler was downed with a devastating shot. "Yes," said the lady, "all the parts we have names for. The parts we don't have names for we grind up and make into bologna, and you Yankees eat it." He must've felt like a federal soldier with a rebel bullethole in the seat of his blue britches.

Now such a thought could very well have turned the outsmarted Yank against bologna eating. And future crossings of the Mason-Dixon line may have been made with trepidation. At least he learned a Southerner's fierce defense of Dixieland is not just a lot of "baloney"!

A couple of spiritual truths are pickled in this briny North-South exchange that may be worth chewing on.

First, a Christian is to have a ready tongue with which to answer questions about his faith. Sensible, sarcastic, or dumb questions—of which there are many. The Bible says, "Be ready always to give an answer to every man that asketh you a reason of the hope that is in you" (1 Peter 3:15). That means have your "gun" loaded with God's Word and shoot straight.

Second, there's a good bit of theology in the marketplace that's a lot of "baloney." When God's truth is ground up and mixed with the devil's lies, the product is "baloney." Trouble is many folks swallow the stuff and think it's good. Theology ought to be checked against the Scriptures to be sure its contents are pure and not an unknown mixture.

When it comes to eternal matters, we'd better go "whole hog" with the Lord. And that's not "baloney."

Pie in the Sky

We called her Mamaw. She was the only grandparent I ever knew, and memories of her are pleasant. Our families lived together for about my first seven years, so that little lady made some indelible marks on me. Like a good grandmother, it was her prerogative to put some spoilin' on her grandchildren. I took to it right well. Some say it was the rotten kind. She kept it up until I was nineteen, when she left us to go live with her Heavenly Father.

Mamaw was a good cook. She knew how to put in a pinch of this, a dab of that, a sprinkle of something else and make it come out some kind of tasty. She could make an egg custard pie of the mouth-waterin' variety. Turned out to be a thing with which to bribe.

When I first started to school, I liked it about as well as a razor-strap whipping. I knew I had to face it, but I would extract a promise from Mamaw. If she'd promise to make me a custard pie, I'd go along peacefully. 'Course I'd have gone anyway, but she figured it would help. Always did. Made the day pass quicker just thinking about what as waitin' for me on the table.

To this day I can't separate Mamaw and custard pie. Think of one and the other comes along. It has something to do with love, promises made and kept, and reward. I knew she loved me, her word was her bond, and she helped me do right by rewarding me. Motivation is what you call it.

Jesus tried to motivate folks to follow Him. There's always a reward waiting. He told a wealthy seeker to give away his earthly riches, "and thou shalt have treasure in heaven: and come follow Me" (Matthew 19:21). Being spiritually near-sighted, he went away sorrowful, choosing earthly riches over heavenly riches.

It reminds me of the time Mamaw had a pot of navy-bean soup on the stove. I dropped in a piece of bread, fished it out and put it between two slices of bread. Now a bean-soup sandwich is soggy and a poor substitute for custard pie.

Saved folks are accused of looking for "pie in the sky in the sweet by-and-by." I wouldn't be a bit surprised to find it so. No, sir, I wouldn't.

A Lesson from Lincoln Logs

Christmas is the time of year when good memories from the past get up and walk around in your head. Sometimes they trigger dormant emotions, causing a smile, a faraway look or even a shiny tear slowly following a crease on an aging face.

Memory can bridge a sixty-year span, or more, as effortlessly as Santa Claus can shinny down a chimney.

Occasionally I recall a ceiling-touching Christmas tree, decorated with dad-placed ornaments, tinsel, and real candles. Under its shelter lay assorted surprises. The happiness and excitement that filled the air, like Christmas Eve stars filling the nighttime sky, play a tune on the heartstrings again. Intermingled are thoughts of the birth of Jesus, without whom Christmas would not be.

Most likely, in those days, presents were fewer but more appreciated than the many in more prosperous times. Then, you were thankful for small favors and treasured them.

As a boy of about six, I found a set of Lincoln Logs under the tree. Dumping them on the floor, I had not the foggiest idea of what to do with them. I knew they were for building things, but at that age, my skills were limited.

Dad understood. He plopped his six-foot frame down beside me and went to work. Piece by piece he put those miniature logs in place. Before my wide-open eyes stood the prettiest little log cabin you'd ever want to see. I was amazed as admiration filled my heart in having such a smart dad. He taught me how to put things together just like the picture-filled instruction book showed. Without his knowledge and patience, I would've been hard put to make any sense out of a pile of disconnected pieces of wood.

Because of my Father's example, I became a pint-sized contractor in the log building business.

That Yuletide memory, like Rudolph's red nose, can be a guiding light. It has to do with building a life, using the available materials which must be assembled. We have an instruction Book—the Bible, and a Master Teacher—Jesus.

In that Book, He said, "Whosoever heareth these sayings of mine, and doeth them, I will liken him unto a wise man which built his house upon a rock." Being storm tested, "It fell not: for it was founded upon a rock" (Matthew 7:24-25).

It's as though Jesus is saying, "Build your life with faith in God, reverence, truth, purity, strong morals, high purpose, honesty. Use only good stuff. And let Me be the foundation." He shows us how to put all of the right pieces in place, resulting in an honorable life well lived, enduring through every storm, and lasting eternally.

Christmas is Christ, the Life-Giver and Builder. Receiving Him is to find the best and most exciting gift of all.

Both Dad and the Lincoln Logs are gone; the lesson remains.

Simply Good

Her name was Aretta. We called her Aunt Retta. Some called her Ret. She originated, lived, and died in the mountains of Kentucky. Starting out as a Jones, she became a Coffey, wife of road builder, Lester. And, like "mountain grown Folgers," there was a good flavor about her. My being a city kid, summertime visits with Aunt Retta were special, as were other mountain visits through the years.

119

Some folks strike that fine balance between being satisfied with having enough and not caring for too many frills. She struck it. Maybe she prayed Solomon's prayer, "Give me neither poverty nor riches" (Proverbs 30:8).

For over sixty years, home for her was a frame house that had stood for over a hundred years. Beneath the shade of huge trees, it had five rooms, a porch, and a "path." Wallpaper, linoleum floor covering and oilcloth on the table gave it a simple attractiveness. A coal stove in the center of the sitting room gave it warmth. Air conditioning was a fan and open windows.

She could've had all of the modern conveniences. Her son, Earl, tried to persuade her, but she didn't want them. Her reasoning was the more stuff you have, the more can go wrong. Being widowed and alone for many years gave her practical wisdom. A car was to ride in but not to own.

Electricity provided light and powered the refrigerator, her one major appliance. She kept the monthly bill low. Water came from the well just outside the kitchen. It became running water when she ran out to get it or when she poured it from the well bucket into the totin' bucket or when it was emptied into the sink with a pipe that ran through the wall to outdoors. The "bathroom" was discreetly located several yards from indoors. The need for a plumber's friend was nil. And seeing as how there was no plumbing, she had to worry about frozen pipes about as much as having an ice storm in the middle of the hot summertime.

Some of the best vittles ever to tickle a palate were cooked on a woodstove. Leftover biscuits and other edibles were put in the warming closets for later consumption. For city slickers, with limited knowledge of woodstoves, warming closets are like little ovens up over the cookstove to keep things warm. Kinda like forerunners to the microwave. The stove was also the water heater.

She wouldn't have a phone. She said people would call to see how she was and wouldn't come to see her. There's that mountain wisdom again.

Always neat and clean, and wearing a fresh apron, she was ready for company to come "set a spell." Expected or unexpected. Conversation was interesting, punctuated with humor. Laughter was as natural as breathing. An often-used word was "pshaw," when some outlandish thing was said. That's like saying, "you don't say."

Some well-meaning social worker might have concluded her to be a deprived mountain woman. Wasn't so. She had everything she wanted and all that she needed. And she was as happy as a lark.

A godly woman, a church-going woman, a woman of sturdy faith in God. In her nineties, she was felled by a fatal sickness. After she was carried from her beloved home to the hospital, her spirit left her earthly tabernacle. She had lived simply, she died quietly. Her heavenly home is like her earthly one: all she needs, all she wants.

Paul said it, Aunt Retta personified it: "Godliness with contentment is great gain. For we brought nothing into this world, and it is certain we shall carry nothing out. And having food and raiment let us be content" (1 Timothy 6:6-8).

There was a simple goodness about Aunt Retta. You might say she was simply good. She had something a lot of folks never find: contentment.

A Frail Giant

Clark Jones, a Kentucky mountain man, was frail in body but with a giant inner strength that had no room for defeat.

When he was a boy, some form of rheumatism became his lifelong companion, gradually bending his body over. Each year he could straighten up less and less. By middle age and beyond, his posture was like that of a half-closed jackknife.

Some people are mastered by their circumstances; others master them. Number Clark among the latter. Possessed with an indomitable spirit, he wore a happy face and walked to the beat of a loving heart. He was as independent as the Fourth of July, not knowing the meaning of a pity party.

On Highway 229, about four miles out of London, Kentucky, stands a small, weather-beaten store. Not a supermarket, but a super market. For Clark was the storekeeper. His smile, neighborliness, and spontaneous laughter made it a good stopping place. Folks tended to stay awhile, gathering around the stove, which stayed put year-round. Even children and young people found in him a friend who listened and cared.

On our trips from North Carolina to Louisville, stopping by to see Clark was as natural as gassing up the car. Memories were woven into our four children's hearts that live to this day. No matter what time it was when we got there, a snack was in order.

A sandwich was made with a slice of bologna thick enough to have two sides. He would ask, "Do you want some salve on it?" That was Clarkese for mayonnaise. A huge slice of onion was optional, making it the deluxe model.

Washed down with a "sody pop" and capped off with some ice cream that simple sandwich made lunch for a happy bunch of children. And all for free. But more than that, Clark's love, hospitality, and generosity were the most important.

He drove his own car, climbed to the top of a burly tobacco barn to make repairs, cut grass, kept house, and did many other things that stand-up-straight folks do.

The secret of Clark's joy was his relationship with Jesus. In late life, he felt the call to preach and attended Clear Creek Mountain Preacher's School for a while. Perched atop a tall stool behind the pulpit, he "ministered the Gospel." He never pastored a church but would preach Jesus whenever he had opportunity.

His tenor singing voice still comes through on a recording he and some cousins made, awakening memories, sometimes accompanied by a tear.

Time came for Clark to move out of the old wooden store. At seventy-four, he moved out of his bent body and into the mansion Jesus said He would prepare. His new body will be arrow straight.

Clark was a personification of God's promise, "My grace is sufficient for thee; for My strength is made perfect in weakness" (2 Corinthians 12:9). And that's encouraging to all who live with some limitation, who depend on God's unlimited help.

Nostalgic Memories

When God created man, He must've programmed the "N" Factor into his nature. Nostalgia. It awakens when something stirs the memory and is often accompanied by emotional response.

We met at Wake Forest College in 1944. Dr. Allen Easley was Professor of Religion and I a young student far away from my Kentucky home. Forty-six years later, we met in his room at the Brookridge Retirement Home. He, nearing a hundred; I not far from seventy. Two elderlies reminiscing. Nostalgia set in.

Not as erect as before, Dr. Easley employs the steadying service of a cane and depends on a pacemaker to strengthen his heart. His mind is tack-sharp, his smile infectious, and his hospitality merits the approval of Emily Post.

Seeing him again rejuvenated memories of events that seemed to have happened only a fortnight ago. We looked at them with pleasure.

This scholarly, now-elder Christian statesman once stood at a crossroads with a then young preacher-boy who needed guidance. His wise council helped to shape my life.

After two weeks at Wake Forest, I wanted to quit and go home. Gently, Dr. Easley said, "Sometimes it's better to stay and master a situation rather than let the situation master you." I stayed. Those words have been an anchor many times since.

Expressing gratitude for the value of his forty-six-year-old advice, I told of using it in sermons. On one occasion I prefaced it with "I'll never forget what Dr. Easley said." Well, sir, my mind took flight, leaving me empty. I strung some rather disjointed words together thereby hoping to save face, but his statement it was not. "Never" is a risky word. However, his laughter at my telling of the blunder made it worthwhile.

Another memory surfaced. Dr. Easley was teaching his class about Noah and the ark. I asked a serious question: "Do you know when money is first mentioned in the Bible?" Admitting his unawareness, I informed the seemingly interested teacher. "When the dove brought the 'greenback.'" He indulged the interruption with a smile and this response: "From the sublime to the ridiculous." Perhaps that's a commentary on life.

As our meeting drew near to a parting, praying together seemed the natural thing to do. Four hands overlapped, two hearts meshed. He asked me to begin. Then he followed with a strong voice of praise, thanksgiving and petition. Our combined prayers were offered in the Name of our Savior, whom we both know and love.

The promise of Jesus was fulfilled: "For where two or three are gathered together in My name, there am I in the midst of them" (Matthew 18:20). No longer were we professor and student but two brothers in the throne room of the King.

My emotional cup was too small to contain the tears, and they spilled over. To briefly hug my mentor of nearly half a century seemed a fitting gesture. God's love was present mightily. With unsteady voice, I said, "I'll see you again," not knowing whether on this side of the river or the other. Either way the promise is true, for our names are inscribed on heaven's roster.

Nostalgic memories are winding paths, along which God's goodness is seen in retrospect. Just another of His gracious blessings.

When Treasures Become Memories

Ornaments and accumulated Christmas decorations were retrieved from their attic storage place. Resting there for a year, it was time for them to add their sparkle and joy to another celebration of the Savior's birth.

Things have to be moved or temporarily stored to make room for the seasonal things of beauty. That's what caused the ensuing heart break.

A grandchild's smiling picture, an antique vase given by a friend, a beautiful little dish and a pretty box of rainbow colored rocks adorned an end table. Placed in a box, they were to be put away so a nativity scene could be displayed.

After Christmas had come and gone and the room was restored, the box of irreplaceable treasures was nowhere to be found. A thorough search produced nothing. The container of precious things must have become part of boxes and paper to be discarded. Though not trash, it was treated, by mistake, like trash.

When something you cherish is suddenly gone, the heart knows the meaning of sadness and remorse. Even tears cannot cause those things to reappear.

That's when treasures become memories. What can no longer be seen with the eyes will then be seen with the heart. God's gift of memory takes over, making the lost treasure permanent, unbreakable, indestructible.

When Jesus said, "Where your treasure is, there will your heart be also," (Matthew 6:21) He was talking about laying up treasure in heaven. Maybe, in the meantime, the heart can be a heaven-like storage room for things once known, possessed or experienced.

Like a family member or a lifelong friend who now walks on eternity's shore. Or a memory-making homeplace, gone due to decay or demolition. Perhaps it's an unrepeatable trip or vacation, the thought of which causes those inner tingles.

It may be that first convertible a car lover once owned and wishes he still had. Or a special doll held close by a little girl. A favorite toy from long ago. A pet that ran away or died. A picture lost in a fire. A piece of jewelry stolen by some heartless thief.

It could be the old meeting house in the country where we were saved, no longer standing but not forgotten. Or that hallowed moment when God became so real it seemed we could almost touch Him.

Everyone has vanished treasures from the past for which he, at times, longs. But they have been gently laid up in the heart. When they float to the surface of our minds, we say, "Why, I remember that!" Precious memories that linger. Aroused, they may be accompanied by a tear or a smile. Precious just the same.

What a lovely and thoughtful thing God has done for us. He knew that we would need the memory of treasures to carry us over some otherwise empty places.

Haunting Memories

Some memories are like the fresh dew of the morning; others arouse that "I wish I hadn't done it" feeling. The facts behind both cannot be erased, only lived with.

One way to deal with the unpleasant ones is to turn them away whenever they clamor for attention. Another way is to try to learn from them, with a determination to avoid falling in that same hole again. And to ask God's forgiveness.

Like Scrooge's unnerving experience when the ghost of Christmas past came to haunt him, a modern-day Christmas memory crops up in my mind every once in a while. It has the right to parade itself in front of me, for I deserve to be haunted.

It was near Christmas, when everyone who can buys a bunch of stuff for folks who most likely have more than they need or can use. It's part of the ritual of the way we celebrate the birthday of Jesus. That's about as near to the real meaning of the original occasion as the star in the east was to earth.

Hurrying toward the big department store, where all of the glittering gifts were displayed to entice shoppers to buy or charge, I had to cross an alleyway. I heard a pleading voice calling out to me: "Boss man?" Glancing in the direction of the sound, I saw an old black man coming toward me. He was far enough away for me to avoid him and to pretend I hadn't heard what I had heard. I was fleet of foot, going on to the warmth and beauty of the great dispenser of Christmas goodies.

Assuming the old man was a beggar, I didn't want to be bothered. I had more important things to do. He may have been hungry or he may have been looking for a friendly face. Since I had no heart of compassion, I'll never know.

Strangely, I can't remember what I bought or even what year it was. But I'm sure my family had a "good Christmas." What I do remember is one word - "Boss man?" and a poorly dressed old man whose cry fell on purposely closed ears. What I could have done, I did not do. The cost would have been little, the reward would have been great.

There are more cries for help in this world than any one person can answer. But there are those special times when a voice penetrates your heart. Many times I have been sensitive to those calls. This time I was not. That memory removed a little wax from my ears so that I can hear more clearly, and it sensitized my heart to the plight of others who may be saying "Boss man?"

Whenever this old ghost floats across my mind, I hear the words of Jesus: "Insamuch as ye did it not to one of the least of these, ye did it not to Me" (Matthew 25:45). What's that, Lord? Were You there in that alleyway? Was that Your voice I heard? Why, I didn't recognize You. Rather, why didn't I recognize You? Did You say, "You weren't looking or listening?"

I wish that scene would just go away. The old man is probably dead by now. I did not have much "silver or gold" to give, but I did have the message of God's love in Jesus that I could have showed and shared. (Could've shared a buck or two along with the good news.) Maybe that's what he needed the most, the showing and telling. I'll never know.

How much better, that in responding to some cry for help, to someday hear Jesus say, "Inasmuch as ye have done it unto one of the least of these My brethren, ye have done it unto Me" (Matthew 25:40).

Hold on there now, He has said it already! A haunting memory need not be wasted.

A Christmas to Remember

Twenty centuries ago the Judean sky was brightened with a star of unusual candle power. Its appointed mission was to pinpoint the location of the Star of heaven who became the Star of Bethlehem—baby Jesus. Among other things, He would bring great joy to all people who believe in Him.

Nearly two thousand Christmases later, eleven-week-old David Harrison Jones celebrated his first Christmas. This little baby also brought joy, along with his handsome little self. Already the birth of Jesus was having a profound influence on him, though he was too young to know.

It happened on this wise. The fifteen of us had finished Christmas dinner. As we sat around the table, carols filled the room, accompanied by the plaintive sounds of the old pump organ. The ageless nativity narrative was read and grateful hearts, united in love, were lifted in prayer. A single candle stood erect on the "Jesus" birthday cake, wick aglow. "Happy Birthday, dear Jesus" completed our offering of praise to the Prince of Peace. Then I noticed something.

Baby David was asleep in his mother Lori's lap. Russell, his dad, was on one side, his Grandpapa on the other, with doting Grandmama next to proud Dad. Cradled in his mother's arms, little David was holding onto Daddy's and Papa's fingers.

Calling attention to the heart-grabbing scene, Russell said, "That's security."

I couldn't help thinking about the security a Christian family has because of Jesus. He holds us, we hold Him, and we are surrounded by God's abundant love. What a safe place to be.

The words of Jesus, like golden jingle bells, echo in our hearts: "I give unto them eternal life; and they shall never perish, neither shall any man pluck them out of My hand" (John 10:28). That's everlasting security, which He alone can give.

My thoughts projected into the future. I visualized a young boy growing toward young manhood, his faith secure in Jesus. Like young Timothy of Bible fame, who had the privilege of being born into a Christian home, the evidence of faith in Jesus was ever before him. Must've been contagious, for it has spread down through the centuries.

Paul gives a thumbnail biography of his youthful friend: "I have been reminded of your sincere faith, which first lived in your grandmother Lois and in your mother Eunice and, I am persuaded, now lives in you also" (2 Timothy 1:5 NIV). Now, a modern-day reenactment of that story is in the making; only the names will be different.

The miracle of Christmas—past, present, and future filled and gladdened our hearts, making it a day to remember. The miracle's name is Jesus.

SECTION 7

Listen To Your Teachers

Stormy Teachers

Storms are predictable and unpredictable. Weather watchers sound warnings, telling where the bad boy is and where he appears to be heading. "Take notice and govern yourself accordingly," the locals are admonished. No one can predict whether a storm will be sound or fury.

At times the would-be predator storm fails to get up a real head of steam. Turns out to be little more than a tempest in a teapot. At other times, he marshals his forces and comes in threatening fashion.

The blue summer sky put on a dark-gray overcoat, trimmed with overlapping collars of fur-like, darker clouds. The sun hid his face, the wind hissed and howled. Lightning-inspired thunder rumbled and rolled. Heavy-handed rain decided to do his thing. The cacophony of sight and sound made uneasiness wrap itself all around. Storms, with broken leashes, can get wild.

Trees expressed obeisance, bending and swaying, curtsying before King Howling Wind. Limbs waved violent howdies. Leaves turned upside down, frantically. Survival depended on the trees strength and root depth.

Observing potential mayhem, I prayed, "O Lord, make the trees strong enough to stand the storm." (A tinge of selfishness may have accompanied the prayer, not wanting the house to get treed.)

Presently the storm took his aggravating self to other unsuspecting areas. Good riddance. And the trees, though bereft of some big twigs and foliage, stopped trembling, and got over their convulsions. They stood the test, becoming stronger because of it. Previous storms helped them endure this one.

Storms are teachers, if viewed with the eyes of the soul. Suddenly, our blue sky turns dark. Dark with trouble that comes with a vengeance. Unexpected sickness, unquenchable pain, irreplaceable loss, heart-tearing sorrow, irreparable brokenness. Dark clothes are their garments. And the wind blows hard. Shoulders stoop, the spirit sags.

Someone prays, "Lord, make them strong to stand the storm." Somehow the trusting soul knows the strength of Jesus is his through the storm. Rightly handled, the severe testing times will make him stronger, and the roots of faith will go deeper.

With Habakkuk, the tested can say, "Although the fig tree shall not blossom, neither shall fruit be in the vines; the labor of the olive shall fail, and the fields shall yield no meat; the flock shall be cut off from the fold, and there shall be no herd in the stalls: Yet I will rejoice in the Lord, I will joy in the God of my salvation" (Habakkuk 3:17-18).

Storms are unpredictable; God is not.

Where Storms Can't Reach

The destination was Louisville, Kentucky. The near capacity loaded Piedmont 737 jet was sixteen minutes late leaving Charlotte, North Carolina. Approaching

Standiford Field in Louisville, we could see ominous clouds. The Captain had announced severe storms were twelve miles from the airport, and we were twelve minutes from landing.

Touchdown. Taxi-ing to the de-loading spot, we prepared to deplane. There being no covered chute for unloading, mobile steps were in place.

Then the twelve minutes and twelve miles locked horns. Seventy-five-mile-per-hour winds were all over the place. Torrential rains soaked everything in sight. Nothing to do but keep our seats. There we sat, with the plane rocking like a big cradle under the hand of a frustrated mama whose baby won't go to sleep.

The 'roused-up elements bullied us for a half-hour or so, then moved on to torment other parts of town. The trail of destruction left thousands without electric power for several days. But no harm had touched us.

A person ought to learn something from what he experiences, else the whole thing is wasted.

There's timing. What if the plane had been a few minutes later? I like to think that God's hand was in it. "My times are in Thy hands," says the Psalmist (Psalm 31:15). That's flight insurance of the finest kind.

Being in the plane was like being secure in the Lord. We were in the storm but protected from its fury. The plane took the wind and rain; we could see limited effects of the storm, without feeling its strength and destruction or hearing its roar.

A stormproof verse says "Your life is hid with Christ in God" (Colossians 3:3). That's a mighty fine place to be when the hurricane force winds of adversity attempt to blow us away.

Prayer was as natural as sparks flying upward. God has a way of filling a place with His Presence when helplessness sets in. Thanksgiving was the dominant note in the song of heart-praise. "It is a good thing to give thanks unto the Lord" (Psalm 92:1). On the tarmac was a heap better place to be than in the swirling winds above ground. The heart said, "Thank You, Lord."

Instinctively we knew the storm would blow itself out. They always do. In life there's more sunshine than boisterous winds. Soon the "all clear" would sound, steps would descend and then reunion with waiting loved ones would take place.

The whole episode is not unlike the Christians journey. Our destiny is heaven. Life is filled with strong winds of opposition, but we are safe in Jesus—kept, protected. The final storm blows over. We ascend to our eternal dwelling place, united with loved ones who got there ahead of us. Best of all, we see Jesus.

"He maketh the storm a calm...He bringeth them unto their desired haven" (Psalm 107:29-30).

Flinderation

A certain section of the Kentucky countryside was the stage on which several tornadoes did a devastating dance. One would drop down, do the twist, and hopscotch yonder.

Our family traveled through the area a few weeks later and stopped to visit relatives.

Naturally the main topic of conversation had to do with the severe damage and the strange happenings which were wrought by the mighty winds.

A dresser drawer, which contained a sleeping baby, was blown into the ground, and a refrigerator had landed on top of it. When the refrigerator was removed, the baby was unharmed. Tiny straws were blown with such force that they penetrated wooden planks on the side of a barn.

In describing all of this, Aunt Retta exclaimed, "It blew everything to flinderation!" I doubt the Weather Service knew about that descriptive word, but it might add a measure of excitement to their reports.

Flinderation usually comes unannounced and unwelcome. Then the "whys" set in. Various views were expressed, seeking to explain the reason for the visit. Some of them were as twisted as the roaring wind itself.

The most severe damage seemed to have been done to a large barn which was filled with hay and cattle. It was said that the wind swept the barn away, and the falling bales of hay killed fourteen cows.

We visited several families in the community and heard the accounts of what happened when the tornado hit the area.

As this was discussed, over and over again we noticed that there was an element of grim satisfaction that divine justice had been wrought. For you see the owners of the barn had ignored the church for years and were known to do farm work on Sunday. Most of the hay in the barn had been gathered on Sunday.

Many of the church-going people of the community looked upon this as God's judgment on unrighteous people. (Couldn't help but wonder if they were the only sinners in the area.)

We traveled on to Louisville where the tornadoes had struck with flinderation power.

Many of the beautiful old trees on the campus of Southern Baptist Seminary lay on the ground, never again to cast their cool shade over the landscape.

Just behind the seminary campus, a section of town where a number of seminary professors lived, lay a scene of utter destruction.

Several professors lost their homes, and one Louisville pastor's home was completely demolished. His wife was severely injured.

Was this God's judgment upon these people? As far as we know, no one in that area of destruction had put up hay on Sunday. Matthew 5:45 says, "He maketh His sun to rise on the evil and on the good, and sendeth rain on the just and on the unjust." That includes tornadoes.

The truth is, there are a lot of things in this world we don't understand. It's best to leave the matter of judging to God "Who judges with righteous judgment."

A bit of innocent humor surfaced during those terrible times. A mother and her little boy went to the basement while the angry wind was at work. When the storm passed over, they went upstairs and saw the wreckage it had caused. The little fella said, "Mama, I did not do it." Seems he had been accused before of flinderation havoc.

In the Day of Judgment, the last thing God wants is for any life to be "blown to flinderation." It is Jesus who makes us flinderation-proof.

A Tidey Tale

There are parables to see in the sea. I saw the restless ocean send its waves onto the waiting beach, then swallow itself again. Nearly every wave brought something with it—dead seaweed, pieces of shell, debris. Sometimes small fish.

Now there's a whale of a difference between objects and fish. One is lifeless; the other has life. The "dead" stuff was washed ashore to stay where it was dumped until a bigger wave moved it again. It had about as much resistance to "current events" as the leviathan had to swallowing Jonah.

But fish are alive and as eager to flop on the beach as a fisherman is to go home with an empty string. Every time the tide would push them near the ocean's edge, they'd make a U-turn and go like an Olympic swimmer for deeper water. It's not the nature of fish to be landlubbers. I saw not one on the beach.

As I paddle-footed around in the water, my mind became a beachhead where a bit of truth landed. I realized life is a lot like what I had seen.

The Bible says those without Christ are "dead in trespasses and sins" (Ephesians 2:1). Dead things don't resist. Like floating seaweed, they are shaped and pushed around by prevailing currents. Like pieces of once-beautiful shells, they are broken by sin's power. Like debris, they are dumped and forgotten.

Proverbs 1:10 warns, "My son, if sinners entice thee, consent thou not!" Constant consenters are as sure to be "all washed up" as the tide is sure to come and go twice a day.

On the other hand, Christians are those fortunate folks whom God "hath raised up...in Christ Jesus" (Ephesians 2:6). And there's as much difference in death and resurrection as in the Sahara Desert and the Atlantic Ocean.

Even Christians sometimes get carried along with the tide. Nearly get beached. But we have a built-in resister. It's called Jesus power—the power of the Holy Spirit. The Bible says, "Resist the devil, and he will flee from you" (James 4:7). In the name of Jesus, we can tell Satan to go jump in the ocean. The Lord gives us "U turn" power and the safety of the depth of God's love. With protection like that, drowning in evil is as likely as landing a shark with a silk thread.

If someone said he saw dead debris become a school of fish, it would sound mighty fishy. But to say that Jesus can take a dead, shattered life and make it live is to tell the Gospel truth.

Bowed but not Broken

The little evergreen shrub (with a shape like a chandelier bulb) had grown to about five-and-a-half-feet tall. Gracing the corner of the house, it exuded its shrubby beauty every season.

Now ol' man Winter can be as tricky as a magician and as surprising as unexpected company. He must've been real sad, because he tuned up and cried all over the place. He dropped his temperature down to the freezing zone. Gradually, those cold, sleet-mixed tears made our part of the world look like a winter wonderland. Icy crystals clung to whatever couldn't shake them off.

Through no fault of its own, the little shrub was forced to don a cold, heavy robe. Being frail, it began to bend beneath the load. By nightfall, its head was resting on the hard pavement. All humped over, it looked like something whipped and defeated, or maybe like it was praying for the cold, dark night to pass.

Made of sturdier stuff than would appear, no branches were broken. Only bent. The suffering shrub, with inbred resiliency, would rise again.

By the next day, Mr. Winter must've caught a little fever. Ice and warmth can't stand each other, so the ice gave up. Just plain disappeared. Late afternoon saw the dripping shrub almost upright, as if to say, "In a while, I'll be as straight and tall as ever. Maybe even stronger than before my testing time came."

It's a parable of life-size proportions. Adversity comes to everyone. Like a winter storm, sometimes it slips up on us. We are caught in the chilling fingers of some uninvited trouble. And we bend beneath its weight.

Presently, our heads bow low, accompanied by a heavy heart. To the casual observer, our posture says defeat. Defeat? Not on your life. We're praying!

Quietly, but surely, the warmth of God's love melts the icy cloak of despair. Reassured that nothing can "separate us from the love of God, which is in Christ Jesus our Lord" (Romans 8:39), we begin to rise. When the wintry blast is over, we stand straight, stronger and with faith-roots deeper than ever.

If God has made a little shrub strong enough to endure crushing loads and then get up, how much more so has He made us.

With the Apostle Paul, we can say, "We are cast down, but not destroyed" (2 Corinthians 4:9). And, like Paul, we find that God's grace is always enough. No matter what.

Warm Hearts in a Cold World

One year, the geraniums in the porch flower box bloomed profusely, beautifying their world with their pastel-pink color. Being sheltered, they survived November's and part of December's chilly nights.

Finally, ol' man Winter doubled up his fist and promised a knock-out punch. Before he could deliver, a few of the remaining blooms were cut, brought indoors, and placed in a vase.

Next morning, winter's blast had done its killing work. Jack had frosted all over the place. Geraniums that were, weren't. Day-before beauty was turned into blight; life was now shrouded in death.

For several days, the blooms that were protected by the warm indoors lived and exuded their beauty. If geraniums could talk, to be sure they would have voiced gratitude. Had it not been for some caring person, they would have been left outdoors to die.

This is a limited parable of life. There are many left-out people in need of shelter in some warm heart. Illustrations abound.

A little unathletic kid knows the pain of always being chosen last, if at all, in a ball game. He remembers the few times when someone gave him a chance and made him feel wanted and needed.

A young man feels shut out and rejected by his father. The longing in his heart to know he's loved goes unfulfilled.

But the years pass; Dad changes. A letter comes with that treasured word "love" in it. Maturity bridges the long-standing gap, and the man understands what the youth could not. Perhaps he was in his dad's heart all along. How nice it would have been if he had only known.

A college lad who had sorta gotten by in high school later goes to college. English was a tough subject for him. A gracious, warm-hearted teacher noticed. Those after-class, private sessions made a difference. She helped bring him out of the cold of ignorance into the warmth of knowledge. Her care will live a lifetime in his appreciative heart.

A husband wounds his wife's spirit by some thoughtless act. He feels shut out of her good graces—and rightly so. Conscience does its gnawing work; repentance and confession join hands. Presently her words of "I forgive you; I love you" oil the door hinges of her heart. It opens, and he's sheltered in the arms of love.

Best of all, no one has to stay out in the cold night of defeated living. For, like the prodigal Son, He can return to his Father's house and hear the joyful words, "This my son was dead, and is alive again; he was lost and is found!" (Luke 15:24).

Through Jesus, there's a glad welcome home in the great heart of God. It is a warm place to be.

A Tale of Two Trees

In the Kentucky mountains stand two formerly magnificent trees that gave shade to an old frame house. They have been part of the landscape for probably a century.

Beneath their outstretched arms and foliage, folks conversed during family reunions or casual neighborly visitation. They were mute witnesses to growing-up children, playing in their shadows.

They gave shelter in times of unexpected rain showers. They heard all kinds of stories that originated in the yard where they were silent sentinels. They had swayed in rhythm to the blowing wind and brought cooling breezes to those sitting on the front porch. Things of beauty were these stately old trees.

The years passed. On the wings of the Spirit, the house dwellers were carried to their heavenly home, leaving the weatherbeaten house vacant. Vacant except for precious memories. There remained the house, with its nearby outbuildings, a well, and the trees. Trees full of life and a willingness to shelter others for years to come.

But things change. New owners took possession of the land, tore the old house down, and built a new, modern one on the same site, next to the veteran trees. It was a new assignment for them. They knew something about sheltering.

Sadly, an irrevocable mistake was made. Instructions that the septic tank lines be laid in the back yard fell on deaf ears. Instead, the trenches were cut in the front yard, cutting the roots of the unsuspecting trees.

Evidence of the fatal blow was not immediately apparent, but before long the trees seemed to cry, "We've been mortally wounded!" Still standing, but with death written all over them, they await removal, to leave a great bare space against the sky. Tragically, they weren't finished living.

My heart ached when I saw them and remembered what they once were, now are, and can never be again. How sad that majestic trees could be felled by tragedy.

These trees are a parable of life. There are persons of radiant Christian character, who, as the Psalmist says, "are like trees planted by rivers of water that bring forth fruit." Without effort, they draw others to themselves. Beautifully, they become a refuge for the weary, a source of comfort for the sad, and like a gentle breeze, the love of God flows from them into the lives of others.

Then, something tragic happens that cuts them down before they are finished with living. Like early morning mist, grief shrouds the hearts of friends who found shelter in those magnificent lives. And now they are gone.

Gone? Thankfully, there is a treetop-tall difference between trees and people. The Bible speaks of another tree. Because Jesus "bare our sins in His own body on the tree" (1 Peter 2:24), the Christian lives eternally.

The life that beautified earth beautifies heaven. The memory of it remains a sheltering place on earth.

A Picture of Humility

Michaelmas Daisies, in late fall, look dead and gone. In the springtime, here they come again. Looking like a third cousin to a tobacco plant gone awry, they grow and grow and grow. Shooting up like Jack's beanstalk, a six-foot man has to look up to see the top.

Tall and as skinny as somebody on a 500 calorie diet, late in the summer they begin to show off. Bedecked with big, beautiful blooms atop their slender stalks, the lavender petals with yellow centers would grace any flower bed. Quietly they seem to say, "Look at me, and I will brighten your day."

This gangly bit of horticulture gets so top heavy it can't hold its head up. Unless staked, it just bows over in a graceful posture. Sometimes even lays its head on the ground. What humility! There one sees the full beauty of its blooming head. It will outlast some of the less hardy plants, blending its color with the turning autumn leaves. Beauty, humility, and endurance all in one.

Several of these uncultivated specimens adorn our driveway. In season, every time we drive up, it's like being welcomed by humble servants whose purpose is to beautify the world. They make coming home a pleasure.

In a sense, to the spiritual eye, these alluring flowers are a reminder of Jesus. An enduring life of beauty and humbleness, He stands taller than anyone the world has ever seen. Not physically, but tall tall. And yet, humility was the flower of His life. He stooped to touch humanity. The Son of God "humbled Himself, and became obedient unto death, even the death of the cross" (Philippians 2:8). And all for us.

What beauty He gives to those who see Him and are drawn to Him. We are told to "be clothed with humility" (1 Peter 5:5), thereby taking on a resemblance to the Humble One. Our role is to give others a glimpse of Him.

The wonder of it all is that God can take ordinary persons, fill them with His Spirit, and grace the world with touches of beauty.

Along the "driveways" of life, a passerby should see in the lives of Christians a spirit of reverence for God and the spirit of servant toward man. That's how it was with Jesus.

To be sure, this drab, old, sad, and hurt-inflicting world would be brighter, happier, and a whole lot safer, if "Michaelmas Daisy" folks cropped up in all directions. Folks who respect God and man. Hospitality would be up, hostility would be down. For there's a lasting, healing beauty about humility. The kind we see in Jesus and in those in whom He lives.

Looking Up

Breakfast is a rather routine affair. One morning it turned out to be an unusually good one - nourishing both body and soul.

The scrambled egg with cheese was palatable. The Smucker's low-sugar-grape-jelly-smeared toast was tasty, and the cold milk washed it down real good. My stomach was as content as a Carnation cow.

For no apparent reason, I looked up. There, within a foot of my nose, was an array of beauty. Three beautiful jonquils in a graceful vase graced the table. The two white ones had their faces turned away from me; the yellow one trimmed in orange was staring at me.

Nestled by the vase was a blue and white speckled ceramic chicken with soulful eyes. In her hollow back were stuffed a bunch of artificial daisies and a white napkin. She looked real pretty. Made me feel like I had company.

Gradually I became aware of the bountiful blessings of our loving Heavenly Father. I was the recipient of so much and the creator of none of it. Truly, "All things are of God" (2 Corinthians 5:18). And consciously I was in His Presence.

All kinds of thoughts filled my mind and spilled over into my heart. I felt that I was at the Lord's table. Gratitude and reverence welled up within me like an artesian well.

Indeed man does not live by bread alone—even with jelly on it. Along with the "vittles," food for the soul is vital. With the eyes of the spirit, one sees through the visible things and finds himself looking at God. Jesus said, "Blessed are your eyes, for they see" (Matthew 13:16).

As long as I looked down at my plate, all I saw was good food with which to break my fast. Ever so close were things of beauty waiting to be discovered. All I had to do was to look up.

Looking up lifts the head and the heart. You have to look up to see mountain tops, stars, the heavens. And best of all, when you gaze heavenward, you just might "see" Jesus.

It's amazing what you can see when you look up.

SECTION 8

Church Happenings

Vestibule of Heaven

In the sand hills of Richmond County, North Carolina, stands a beautiful, white, country church. Cartledge Creek Baptist Church has been a meeting house since the early 1800s. On Heaven's roster are the names of those who found the Lord because of this church. Only God knows the total tally. Hallowed are the memories of this sacred spot.

Upon seminary graduation, it became our first pastorate, one of two half-time country churches.

This story tells the highlights of the moving of the Holy Spirit in the life of a man named Marvin.

Marvin, his wife, and several small children moved into the community as tenants. Sawmilling was his occupation. Their home reflected the results of his drinking, making him a poor provider. His cruelty was reflected in the faces of his wife and little children. Happiness was not known there; misery was.

Some in the community had tried to help this family but had given up. Even a church leader said, "I'll speak to him, but I'll have nothing to do with him." His life was so terrible that he made himself a social outcast.

Invitations to come to church and Gospel sharing seemingly bore little fruit. Not yet, anyway. My visits to the home created a friendship. On one such visit, Marvin was not there. In a drunken stupor, he had driven his old Model A Ford into a mud hole not far from the house. I found him. Embarrassed, he said, "Ain't I a pretty sight?"

Getting behind the stuck A Model, I pushed, while he navigated. I said aloud, "Push, Lord!" Not exactly a proper pulpit kind of prayer, but I needed all the help I could get. The good Lord heard my plea. My red-mud-covered shoes must've weighed about ten pounds. Anyhow, the car got unstuck.

Maybe, just maybe, the Lord used that episode to reach into this needy man's muddy heart. A change was in the making. After a while, he and his family started attending church.

On a bright Sunday morning, Heaven's brightness would shine within the walls of Cartledge Creek Church. Marvin, clean and dressed in a white shirt that had been given to him, came to church, family in tow. At the sermon's close, an invitation to receive Christ as Savior was given.

Marvin, with face glowing, walked down the aisle, arms outstretched. Jesus had won the victory, and the church rejoiced. It was my joy to baptize him in a nearby pond. His life changed. Drinking was a thing of the past. He had a clean heart and a clean house. There was a new reflection in the home—the glory and grace of Jesus.

We both moved away from the community. He and his family came to visit. It was a time when we could share together as brothers in Christ.

Some years later, a letter came from his wife. In it she said, "Marvin is still living for the Lord." Time to rejoice again.

Our paths have not converged for over thirty years. We may not see each other again this side of heaven. But what a day it will be when our Savior's face we shall see. Together, we will praise Him forever!

Marvin is proof of the promise Jesus made, "Him that cometh to me I will in no wise cast out" (John 6:37).

Cartledge Creek Baptist Church. Why, it must be the vestibule of heaven!

Touch of Glory

"Where the Spirit of the Lord is, there is liberty" (2 Corinthians 3:17). We found this to be true at Emerald Isle Chapel by the Sea.

The genial pastor, Wales native Leslie Thomas, met my wife and me in the church yard. With genuine sincerity and a beaming smile, we were welcomed to prayer meeting. Already we were happy with our decision to attend. Most of the folks were greeted with a gentle hug and all with a spirit of "I'm glad you came."

By human counting, the attendance was small. By celestial reckoning, it was a big meeting. Jesus said, "Where two or three are gathered together in my name, there am I in the midst of them" (Matthew 18:20). And among us He was. We realized again that you can be among total strangers who are not strangers at all. They become friends immediately and kinsmen in the Lord. Our binding friendship with Jesus binds us to one another.

There was liberty in the service, not license to do as you please, but the liberty of the Holy Spirit directing.

We sang. While singing "For You I Am Praying," we were asked to visualize the face of someone who

157

needed our prayers. The song took on new meaning. Someone somewhere received a blessing.

We prayed. Unhurriedly. Several prayed aloud for the spoken requests—ranging from spiritual needs to physical. We knew God was listening—with answers.

A couple of young men sang Gospel songs, accompanied by a guitar. One had been rescued from a tragic life of sin. Looking at their faces convinced us they knew Jesus of whom they sang. Pure joy. There was no conflict between the hymn book songs and theirs. All were offered to the Lord as an offering of praise.

We were taught from God's Word—Romans 10. The pastor told us of the impossibility of man's establishing his own righteousness. However, God has made the righteousness of Christ available to all who confess that Jesus is Lord and believe in Him in their hearts (Romans 10:9-10). We rejoiced again in the assurance of our salvation.

After the benediction, sharing with each other continued, until final goodnights and "God bless you." With gladdened heart and a bit of hesitation, we left The Chapel by the Sea, looking forward to another time with God's people in God's house.

Could this be a little foretaste of heaven? "For now we see through a glass, darkly; but then face to face" (1 Corinthians 13:12),

Worship Can Be Lively

Man's ways of worshiping God are as varied as Heinz Fifty-seven Varieties. All the way from stoically calm to somewhat on the boisterous side. And many shades in between.

Usually folks are sincere regardless of the tack their worship takes. Depends a lot on the emotional makeup, coupled with understanding.

Cousin Earl shared some "church history" originating in the mountains. His pre-believing days as a young man were not of the sanctified sort.

He and his musical friends were often invited to play their guitars, mandolins, and fiddles for church services— especially revivals. Shouting and aisle-traipsing were not uncommon on occasion.

Lively sacred songs would help get things going. Then, without the congregation suspecting, the music makers, for pure devilment, would swing into "The Chinese Breakdown." I take it that wasn't exactly a Christian song; but the ones praising the Lord were so caught up, it didn't matter.

He tells a couple of tales about Kinkey Jr. Church. Kinkey Church is on top of a mountain; Kinkey Jr. is a piece down the road.

All kinds of disruptive things were done to add spice to the services. Like throwing a cat through the window. I don't know if that had the same effect as Ray Stevens's "Mississippi Squirrel Revival" or not, but I 'spect it livened things up a bit. The bewildered feline wasn't thrown in to get converted, but he might have scared the devil out of some who hadn't considered their eternal destiny with much seriousness.

On another occasion, a man got turned on. Running all over the church house, he yelled, "I feel so good I could run a mile." Some statements are figurative but taken literally. One obliging brother hollered "Open the door and let him out!"

The exuberant brother was in no mood to express his love for the Lord that extensively, so he took a seat in the Amen corner.

Now the Bible says, "When thou vowest a vow unto God, defer not to pay it" (Ecclesiastes 5:4), but this revved-up worshiper hadn't exactly made a vow. Actually, he hadn't said he would run a mile, just that he could. So he reneged. Anyway, the Amen corner was a better place to be than tearing down the road making folks wonder what was after you.

However a person worships the Lord, at least he worships. He may be as motionless as a wooden Indian, or he may whoop a little. Either way is a sight better than never worshiping at all.

"O come, let us worship and bow down: let us kneel before the Lord our maker" (Psalm 95:6).

Amen.

Puffy and Huffy

Folks don't always say what they really mean. A guileless person may take a statement as straight talk only to discover it was as curved as a pitcher's tricky pitch.

It's not uncommon for a few curves to be thrown among church folks. A spiritual babe (1 Corinthians 3:1) may talk like he wants to "sit on the bench" when he really wants to be manager. He's "vainly puffed up by his fleshly mind" (Colossians 2:18). He's what you might call a puffy Christian. You can't tell it by what he says at first, but it comes out at last.

A preacher told of a man in an early pastorate he served. Brother "Puffy" had been Sunday School Superintendent since the ark settled on Mt. Ararat. Every year he offered his resignation; and as he knew it would be, it was rejected. It was a church ritual and his annual vote of approval. Did wonders for his ego.

The preacher being new, the Super made his pitch: "I've been the Sunday School Superintendent for many years. I think it's time for me to step down and let someone else have it."

Taking his humble words at face value, the gullible parson put his arm around the old man's shoulder and commended him for his decision. And so the transition was made.

Assuming that all was well, the preacher was about to learn that a curve ball had zinged over the plate. And he had taken a mighty swing at it. Instead of making a home run, he had fallen flat on his ministerial face.

Later the puffy brother got huffy - as huffy as a settin' hen yanked off her nest. "Preacher, you put me out of being Sunday School Superintendent." To which the bewildered reverend replied, "Now wait a minute. You came to me and said you thought you should step aside and let someone else have the job." Truth was about to emerge. "Yes, but you agreed with me!"

He had had about as much intention of letting go his hold on his position as a wrestler his hammer-lock on his opponent. The sound of his words and sound of his heart were as close as the front pew is to the back pew.

Our words ought to express our intentions. Too often like the Psalmist said: "The words of his mouth were smoother than butter, but war was in his heart" (Psalm 55:21).

I reckon the church would fare better if folks would say what they mean and mean what they say. Sure would cut down on a lot of deception done in the Name of the Lord.

A Sweet Revival

Since I was the new parson at the church, it was decided I should be the revival preacher. It's something of an honor to do that in your own church. Besides, it's cheaper than an imported prophet - no meals, lodging, or honorarium. Lots of honor but no honorarium. You might call him a no-profit-Prophet. Except for the Lord's promise that His word would "not return unto Him void" (Isaiah 55:11), the revival was a little on the duddy side. No headline screamed of outstanding success. Fact is, more folks were "out standing" somewhere else than in the meeting house.

In his younger days, a preacher has delusions of grandeur as to his prowess as a preacher. Apt as not it'll turn out to be an illusion. Seems that's what happened in this particular protracted meeting. The folks that were supposed to stream down the aisles forgot to stream.

A revival that doesn't revive has a devastating effect on the evangelist's spirit. Makes his head droop. He flagellates himself and feels sackcloth and ashes should be his lot. He just knows something must be wrong with him that hindered the Spirit from working.

Now while walking through despair's valley, I was sharing my disappointment with a nice lady church member. Her words of reassurance were calculated to lift up the fallen: "I think we had a real sweet revival." Didn't so much as get me off the floor.

I thought to myself, "That's what we had—a real sweet revival. Nobody got mad, nobody repented—visibly, nobody got saved, and nobody rededicated." We just had us a good ol' time in church but didn't give the angels much cause for rejoicing.

There's as much difference in a meeting and a revival as dipping your finger in a finger bowl and in taking a bath. God's people have to want a real cleaning before much happens. Like the psalmist, we must cry, "Wilt Thous not revive us again: that Thy people may rejoice in Thee?" (Psalm 85:6). Or like Habakkuk, the prophet, "O Lord, revive Thy work in the midst of the years, in the midst of the years make known: in wrath remember mercy" (Habakkuk 3:2). That kind of praying gets the Lord's attention, and the dews of heaven water our souls.

God says we have to humble ourselves, pray, seek His face and turn from our wicked ways for Him to hear, forgive and heal (2 Chronicles 7:14). There's more agony in that than sweetness, but a fellow will know something's happened.

Maybe the Lord spoke to me that day through the kind lady to let me know He did more than I could tell. I hope He did. I really do.

Deaking Deacons

The idea of deacons is God's. Men were chosen to serve as deacons because of murmuring in the early church (Acts 6:1-4). The office has continued ever since. (So has the murmuring.) The problems haven't always been solved, though valiant efforts have often been made.

For the most part, my dealings with deacons have been on the pleasant and profitable side. Occasionally some have contributed to the whiteness of the follicles on my scalp. Doubtless, I have helped a few of their heads to whiten up considerably, too. That seems par for the course, but God's grace ruleth over all.

At times, deacons' meetings can be about as peaceful as a political caucus. Maybe the good Lord steps outside and waits for them to slug it out before re-entering. I heard of such a meeting.

A preacher-friend told of a time when his deacons had a real "knock-down-drag-out" session. The issue was not revealed, the antics were. Most of the time issues are forgotten anyway. It's the other stuff that remains.

At the close of the meeting, the deacon-team was about as together as a team of mules pulling in different directions. "Love for the brethren" was a mite on the strained side. Fortunately, the Lord seems always to have someone on hand whose speech is "always with grace" (Colossians 4:6). Only this time "grace" was of a different brand.

In the group was a man who spoke plainly and talked with the Lord on earthly terms. He may have been a veteran of church wars. Foreign wars, that is; for such wars are foreign to the Lord's ways.

He was pressed into service for the closing prayer. Prayed he, "Lord, we thank Thee that we could meet here tonight where we could discuss, fuss, and almost cuss."

Well, sir, that was like turning the cat around and rubbing his fur the right way. Tensions melted like margarine in the sun. I understand that the "spiritual leaders" went away with a reduced head of steam. May have even saved the church from a civil war.

As a child, daughter Hannah saw several mules in a corner of a field with their heads together. Innocently she said, "They must be having a deacons' meeting." I'll not try to unravel the connection in her mind. I only know that when God's men get their heads and hearts together, they can pull like mules toward a common destination—a Spirit-filled church.

Let the deacons deak!

Approaches and Landings

A right approach is real helpful if the plane is to hit the runway properly. Likewise is witnessing. Sometimes we are made to feel we didn't even come close to making a landing. Could have something to do with the approach we made.

I recall a prospect who was about as spotless as a leopard. You name it, he'd done it. He was the kind Jesus is always hunting, offering treasures of forgiveness and eternal life. Thought sure this lad with the loused-up life would welcome the chance to come clean. What approach I used must've been as effective as trying to sell life insurance to the deceased. After explaining the need for and the advantage of receiving Jesus as Savior, I asked him the crucial question: "Will you accept Christ now?" The Bible warns, "How shall we escape, if we neglect so great salvation?" (Hebrews 2:3), so it's about the most pertinent thing you can point at someone.

Now his response indicated he wasn't aware that his soul's house was on fire. "No," he said, "I can't do that right now." Being nosey, I let him explain. "I may go to the hospital." The mystery thickened. "What does accepting Christ have to do with your going to the hospital?" Seemed a logical inquiry. He said, "Well, I've got some more fighting to do, and I don't know whether I'm going to end up in the hospital, or the other guy." Guess he knew Jesus would take the fight out of him, and he wasn't ready for that just then. He was as evasive as a hockey puck.

Times are when we sense the landing strip is "over there," and we end up in the trees. Paul may have felt that way since he didn't land all of his prospects, either. Governor Felix got right nervous when Paul "reasoned of righteousness, temperance and judgment to come" and said, "Go thy way for this time, when I have a convenient season, I will call for thee" (Acts 24:25). The record doesn't say that he ever took hold of what Paul told him about Jesus. He couldn't say, though, that he never heard. Even King Agrippa said, "Almost thou persuadest me to be a Christian" (Acts 26:28). Seems that one missed it, too.

Who knows, though? We may have come closer to a good landing than we know now. Some happy person may greet us in heaven that we thought landed on the lower runway. Even a sloppy approach is better than none.

Ready to Die—Beginning to Live

It happened on a Tuesday. In response to a concerned wife's request, I went to see her nearly 66-year-old husband. A good man, but not saved. He was the object of his wife's love and prayers for the 17 years of their marriage.

A pleasant visit it was, getting acquainted through general conversation, exchanging pleasantries. The pet parrot was a focal point as he added to the chit-chat. But my purpose superseded all of this.

Admitting that he did not know the Lord as his Savior, my new friend seemed hungry of heart to know Him. Together we walked through the story of God's love, the death of Jesus for our sins, and His resurrection. When asked if he would like to receive Jesus as his Savior, his answer was "yes." The transaction was sealed with a prayer. There was praise and thanksgiving.

Tears of joy gleamed in the eyes of a patient and loving wife.

The following Sunday, he was with her in church. At the close of the service, he came to the front of the auditorium to make public what had transpired in the privacy of his home and heart. And the church rejoiced, along with the angels in heaven.

On Sunday, February 23, Maynard Jones was baptized into the fellowship of Salem Baptist Church. It was the last Sunday of my being interim pastor. What a climax! We share the same name, and by sharing the same Savior, we now are brothers.

Four of his brothers and two sisters joined other family members to witness Maynard follow Christ in believers baptism—a picture of the death, burial, and resurrection of Jesus. The family circle was complete.

Eighteen gathered at the Jones' home for Sunday dinner. A happy time. The subject of being ready to die came up. Maynard made a memorable comment: "I'm ready to die, but I'm just beginning to live." Why, he might even start singing, "What a wonderful change in my life has been wrought, since Jesus came into my heart!"

The words of Jesus come to mind: "Whoever liveth and believeth in Me shall never die" (John 11:26). Maynard knows he is now one of the Lord's born again ones. For the first time in his life, he is alive unto Jesus Christ his Lord.

Walking with Jesus is a progressive, upward walk, abundantly joyful along the way; and, as the old song says, "The way of the cross leads home." Our heavenly home.

Home is where Maynard and all believers, who love the appearing of the Lord, will be given a crown of righteousness (2 Timothy 4:8). It will fit just right. Jesus will say, "I laid this up for you the day you invited Me into your heart."

The redeemed of the Lord will contemplate the cost of that beautiful crown: the precious blood of Jesus. And we will remember the cost to us: the willingness to show the white flag of a surrendered will to the One who conquered us with His love.

Invitations and RSVPs

The sermon concludes and the invitation is extended. That's standard procedure in most Baptist churches. It's a time when the preacher hopes someone will make a decision. No matter what the invitation hymn is, too many folks seem to sing under their breath, "I shall not be moved."

Occasionally an unusual response is made to the parson's pleadings. It may be about as close to what he has in mind as overalls being appropriate apparel for a White House dinner. Sometimes it's hard to stifle the snickers, so he just smiles inwardly and receives the responder reverently.

I remember a lady who came forward one Sunday. The preacher is always glad to get an RSVP to his invitation, but her reason for coming was concern for a friend. I think her "tang got toungled" up when she said, "I'd like for you to pray for a friend of mine in the restroom." To be sure, she meant rest home. Having made her intercessory request, she returned to her pew—leaving the preacher grinning to himself. I'm sure the Lord understood her and him.

Then there was another time. Hospital emergencies on a Saturday included my sick mother-in-law, a wreck fatality's grieving family, and a coal miner dying with black lung without Christ. Trying to help these folks deepened my conviction that knowing Jesus is imperative. That Sunday, I preached with urgency. Did about the best I knew how to do and just knew folks would answer the altar call. Lots of them.

Now I reckon there are times when flesh takes precedence over spirit. The only response to all of that mighty preaching was a good brother with a pressing problem. With our hands joined in holy welcome, he laid his request on me. "My bladder's stopped up. Will you pray for me?" Here I was, fervently reaching for souls and I got a bladder instead.

To say the least, that's about the funniest thing that ever happened to me at invitation time. In all fairness to the sincere responder, he did make a rededication of his life to the Lord who has power to move heaven and earth. Including bladders.

Now this didn't do a thing for my hopes of a great outpouring of revival that day. I felt about as successful as a Fuller brush salesman whose sales for the day were zilch.

No matter how unusual our responses may be to God's invitation, Jesus keeps on saying, "Come unto Me, all ye that labor and are heavy laden, and I will give you rest" (Matthew 11:28).

We may give Jesus reason to smile at us, but He won't laugh at us. He cares about rest homes, bladders, souls, and whatever else that troubles His friends.

Inspiration

Memorable moments of inspiration crop up unexpectedly. Often the inspirer is totally unaware of the emotional response he has triggered.

It happened at the Evangelistic Conference, February of 1990. That's the annual gathering of preachers, singers, and other folks somehow related to the heavenly calling of Gospel proclamation.

Now some preachers are happily situated, while some are hoping for a shot at grazing in the proverbial greener pasture. Some are dragging as low as a dachshunds underside, some are gratefully retired, while others are as tired as a man who misplaced his Geritol, and some have been "pink slipped."

Meandering through the corridors, howdying with one another, is part of the ritual. Some of us need to wear the lapel button which truthfully declares, "Hi! I can't remember your name either." But we traipse to the big meeting each year, with hopes as high as a kite. It's inspiration time.

We go to get our spiritual engines revved up by the turbocharged dynamo preachers. We want somebody to kick in the afterburners to lift our heaven-bound hearts into orbit. We listen for music that will cause soul tremors of Richter Scale magnitude. Most of the times we go away with the dew of heaven dripping all over us, saying, "What a meeting!"

Without the aid of tapes, a minimal amount of the audio is recalled. But my eyes took in something that slipped right down into my heart.

On the very front row of the ground-level seats was a boy I would judge to be about ten or eleven, sitting with one I assumed to be his dad. A good-looking kid, clean cut, with neatly-trimmed light-brown hair. He was wearing a brown- and-yellow jacket with USA in bold letters on it.

I noticed how intently he listened to the preachers. He sang from memory, "Victory in Jesus," "The Lily of the Valley," and "What a Friend We Have in Jesus." Accompanied by timekeeping clapping, he joined in "This Is the Day the Lord Has Made." He looked happy.

This dad could well echo the words of the Father about His Son, "This is my beloved Son in whom I am well pleased."

Without trying, that little lad was showing evidence of a Christian home, Sunday School, church, good training, a love for Jesus, and reverence and respect for God and country. Following the benediction, he was seen following obediently in his father's footsteps. I saw them no more, except when looking into my heart. What I heard will fade; this scene will not.

I kept thinking: what if all children could be loved into the Kingdom of God like this little fella is? And I saw again the beautiful difference Jesus makes in those who know Him as Savior.

Son, you lit the fire of inspiration in my heart that day. Thank you and God bless.

Service Beyond Duty

Before the Lord returned to heaven, He told His disciples to "go into all the world, and preach the gospel to every creature" (Mark 16:14). That "into all the world" can get a person into some right precarious places.

I met the man for the first time in jail. (He was on the inside of the bars, I was on the outside.) In fact, most of the times I saw him were like that. He was as quick to break the law as nursery rhyme's nimble Jack was to "jump over the candlestick." Knowing he was one of the "every creatures" the Lord mentioned, I shared the good news with him at 'most every opportunity. He was as responsive as any man would be who wanted to get "sprung." It never seemed to change his ways much, but at least he heard the good Word.

One day he summoned me to his cell. Had a request. Having written a letter to his hospitalized wife, he asked me to deliver it. The only hitch was she was not able to read. That meant I was to be like the singing telegram boys. So far so good.

Now the wife's bed was in the hospital corridor, with right much traffic passing by. Drawing my chair near her bedside, I began reading. I almost choked when I saw nearly every paragraph began with "Honey." And a lot of gooey stuff was interspersed throughout the epistle—like "Honey, I miss you," Honey, I love you." There were other phrases that have mercifully slipped my mind. I started to skip the word but felt it would be unfair. After all, it was a love letter, and they're supposed to be sweet.

About that time, I sorta wished the Lord had called me to dig ditches or something less hazardous. I felt that I deserved the Bronze Star or a medal of some kind for "Service Beyond the Call of Duty." If some of my church members had passed by and heard me honeying the lady and telling her I loved her, I probably would have been eligible for the Purple Heart. Anyway, my face felt plum purple.

You might say I was heeding the word of the Lord, "Watch and pray" (Mark 14:38). I kept my eye pealed for nosey visitors and prayed that none would happen along. Was I evermore relieved when that bit of ministerial ministering was done!

When the Lord says, "Whom shall I send, and who will go for us?" we'd better be careful in saying, "Here am I; send me" (Isaiah 6:8). He just might send us to jail or to a bedside with a honey letter.

Horse Sense

Colleges don't grant degrees in horse sense. Neither is it acquired like learning math. It's more like a sixth sense that some folks seem to have more of than others. Wise response to situations has a lot to do with a person's gaining the reputation of having this desired commodity. Another term for it is strong common sense.

At a horse show in Atlanta, GA, a horse trainer, in western garb, and an unridden, unbridled mare squared off. The pen was a circle; the process of breaking the mare was called Round Pen Reasoning. And 'round and 'round they went, as "reasoning" took place.

When the man got behind the mare, she would run like the wind. When he stood in front, they just eyeballed one another. Then he would touch, pat, and stroke her and back off. Kinda like getting acquainted. With each approach, he made a calming, clucking sound, which may have been horse talk.

The bridle was held up for her to see, followed by more patting and retreating. Then he touched her with the bridle and stepped back. The routine was repeated, until she allowed him to slip the bridle over her head.

Next came the saddle blanket and saddle. She was a little skittish. His tactic of approaching, touching, and backing off was repeated numerous times. Finally, she stood there, a well-dressed mare in bridle and saddle.

Time came to mount up. Same process. First, a little weight in the stirrup, then stepping back. More patting. Gradually, his whole weight was in the stirrup, and Miss Mare didn't object.

Within two hours, the trainer was in the saddle, on a horse that never before had had such an oddity astraddle her back. He didn't stay there long. He said, "If a horse moves the front feet and does not move the back feet, it's fixing to buck." Sensing this, he knew he was about to wear out his welcome. Dismounting was the prudent thing to do. More getting acquainted time would cure the situation.

The secret of the "Taming of the Mare" was establishing a relationship, winning confidence, and showing patience, kindness, gentleness. That's horse sense. The trainer earned the right to occupy the saddle. The horse allowed him to be there.

Preachers could learn a lot by using the same kind of horse sense with their congregations.

A preacher ought not to come swaggering onto a church field, wearing spurs, and carrying a bullwhip and a lariat. Neither should he be rough-handed nor have a trail-boss "move 'em up, head 'em out" mentality. He should remember his calling is to be a shepherd and not a cowboy. To forget this is asking to be bucked off, before he gets settled in the saddle.

Using horse sense, the preacher can win the confidence and love of his folks. They give him the privilege of being their pastor. They also have the power to unseat him but are not apt to, if they know he loves them. Otherwise he may become a "pastureless pastor."

Finding himself in difficulty and having been thrown, a preacher needs to let the Spirit bear His fruit of "love...patience...kindness...gentleness" through him (Galatians 5:22). That's spiritual horse sense. Then he just might get to sing Gene Autry's old song: "I'm Back in the Saddle Again...Come A-Kai-Yai-Yippy, Yippy-Yay!!"

That's horse sense set to music for PRAISE THE LORD!

We All Make Failures

With unsteady steps, a fellow-sinner entered my office. John Barleycorn makes a man walk crooked and befuddles his mind. His reasoning gets as tangled as spaghetti, and even lines of Scripture might get switched. The Book reads, "Be not drunk with wine, wherein is excess; but be filled with the Spirit" (Ephesians 5:18). But bleary eyes could see it, "Be not filled with the Spirit, wherein is excess, but be drunk with wine." My visitor seemed to have made his own translation.

It's pitiful to see a man of potential blow it. Must grieve the Lord something terrible. He finally gets to the "can't stand himself" place, and lashes out at anybody within lashing distance. He saddles them with blame for his self-inflicted wounds. It's hard for a man to say "I've gone and paddled up the wrong creek." That'd get too close to repentance.

Counseling success seemed about as near as the moon. Being a mite fretted with accusations and innuendoes (whatever those things are), I began feeling like a kid with an "F" on his report card. I knew there was a seeking soul down in there somewhere, but a likkered-up man is tough to reach.

I stood up and hoped he'd take the hint that it was time to go. It was then he hit me with a prayer request. He even told me what to pray. Nothing to do but hunker down and lay hold on the horns of the altar. Did about as good a job of beseeching the Lord as I knew how. I even tattled on the poor guy sitting there. Maybe it would help the Lord understand the situation. I rebuked the devil, commanded him to turn loose, and hoped he'd go back to the hot, nether world where he belonged. He didn't.

Rising with a hopeful feeling, I was informed I hadn't got it right in my prayer. Exasperatedly I exclaimed, "Well, I failed again! I can't even pray right!" I hoped that would sober him up a little and shame him some. Might even get the struggling reverend a dab of compassion.

His reply made me think he had found a measure of comfort: "Well, we all make failures."

Then the truth hit me: he was right. The Bible says, "All have sinned and come short of the glory of God" (Romans 3:23). That lumps all of us drunk sinners and sober sinners together. Getting plastered is not my failure, but I realized that there are many other imperfections (fancy word for "sins") with which I am required to deal.

About that time, shame for my own failures took over. God has His ways of bringing us down off our highhorse.

Jesus was accused of associating with sinners, for which we are eternally grateful. That's good news for all of us.

Admitting our failures, we pray, "It's *me*, it's *me*, O Lord, standin' in the need of prayer!"

Learning to Preach

Preaching is supposed to be a calling, not a mere profession. Some preachers seem to be more gifted in expounding the Word and exhorting the rapt listeners than others. (Some listeners are more rapt in listening than others, some don't give a rap.)

This (embellished) preacher yarn was told many years ago by Earl Guinn at an evangelism conference.

A young fellow felt the call stirring in his soul. He announced the good news to his mama: "Mama, I've been called to preach." She was pleased, but knew some schooling was required.

Mama's counsel was, "Well, Son, if you've been called to preach, you'll have to go to school to learn how to preach." Seemed the reasonable thing to do, so off he went.

Two weeks later, he was back home. Mama said, "Why'd you quit?" "I didn't quit: I learned how to preach," was his reply. "Well," she said, "if you learned how to preach, preach for me a little bit."

Rather unenthusiastically, the novice proclaimer started out: "The hound dog chased the rabbit in the hollow tree." Somewhat disappointed, Mama responded, "Son, that's not preaching. You'll have to do better than that. Try it again."

This time he was determined to show his mama education had paid off. Loading his lungs to the gills, assuming a ministerial stance and turning his voice volume up to about seventy-five decibels, he let 'er rip, bellowing like Blaylocks's bull: "O-UH, THE-UH HOUND DOG-UH CHASED THE RABBIT-UH IN THE HOLLOW TREE-UH!"

Mama was as pleased as punch. With an approving smile and affirmative nod, she gushed, "Why, Son, I believe you have learned how to preach!" She now had her a preacher-boy, ready to do combat with the devil and all his angels.

The obvious point of the story is that it's not what you say, it's how you say it. That kind of preaching falls in the category of a person's evaluation of a certain sermon. Like when a man was asked if he thought the Lord had given the preacher the message, he replied, "The Lord didn't give him nothin' but the wind."

Regrettably, there's a good bit of preaching which is mostly wind without much substance. A preacher friend told of the response by one of his church members to a sermon he had preached. "I enjoyed your sermon. It didn't have no doctrine in it ner nothin'."

When the Prophet Jeremiah was called to preach, the Lord said, "Behold, I have put my words in thy mouth" (Jeremiah 1:9). He also said, "I will make my words in thy mouth fire" (5:14). Later the faithful preacher said, "His Word was in mine heart as a burning fire shut up in my bones" (20:9). What a preacher! Something to say and a burning desire to say it.

That kind of preaching may not have much effect on hound dogs, scared rabbits, and hollow-tree-refuges, but it sure can set fire to the sin in a person's heart and help him find refuge in the arms of Jesus. When the preacher, filled with the fire of the Holy Spirit, sees that happen, he can say, "Mama, I'VE LEARNED TO PREACH!"

Tug of War

A question asked may not bring the anticipated answer, turning a supposedly serious moment into laughter.

It happened at prayer meeting. The Bible study centered on the Prophet Isaiah's vision of God (Isaiah 6). Seeing the glory and holiness of the Lord, Isaiah lamented, "Woe is me! For I am undone; because I am a man of unclean lips." In light of God's perfection, he became aware of his wretchedness.

The question: "What would your reaction be in finding yourself in the presence of someone clean, well-groomed, and well-dressed, and you dirty, wearing old clothes and hair disheveled?"

With appropriate gestures, a man gave an unexpected reply: "I'd want to slap him and shake him so he would look as bad as I look!"

That wasn't exactly what I had in mind. Of course, the responder said it with tongue-in-cheek. It was a bit of comic-relief, adding a memorable moment that served as backdrop to the real response of humility before the Lord.

There's truth a-plenty in that quick-on-the-draw answer: mankind is good at trying to bring God down to its level. It's supposed to make self look better but works about as well as putting a cutaway coat, striped trousers, a tall silk hat, and spats on an unwashed hobo. Lifting is God's intention. He never accommodates Himself to our standards.

A few examples illustrate.

For "the man downstairs" to refer to God as "the Man upstairs" makes God perceived to be like a celestial version of Clark Kent - Superman.

When people, with closed hearts, accused Jesus of having a devil, it was their feeble attempt to make Him no better than themselves.

An atheist (who no doubt had never been in a foxhole) looked heavenward and said, "If there is a God, let Him strike me dead in five minutes." He was trying to put himself as far above God as the stars are above the earth. The denial of his request only proved God's patience with blindness, not His non-existence. He's not One who reacts to man's manipulativeness.

Now, back to Isaiah. Through confession and cleansing, he found himself high and lifted up into God's Presence. He became who he was meant to be. It worked then; it works now.

Jesus specializes in lifting people. Like the time He forgave a caught sinner and then said, "Go and sin no more." Or the times He lifted some little children up and gave them His blessing. Or when He healed a man of his blindness and commended his faith. He's the Great Encourager to all who look up to Him.

"Him that cometh to Me I will in no wise cast out" (John 6:37), says the One who reaches down to those who want to be lifted up. That lifting puts us on a heavenly journey that lasts eternally.

Incredible!

A Fist or an Extended Hand?

The preacher's wife, Harriett, was leading the children in "Preacher's Children's Church." That's the time when the little folk come to the front to hear a story.

Sharing a story out of her son's life, when he was in grade school, brought an unexpected response.

Russell had a declared enemy who threatened to beat him up. The threat was repeated each day on their way home from school.

Harriett asked the children, "Have any of you ever had someone threaten to beat you up?" One little boy raised his hand as high as it would go, waving it back and forth. He knew what she was talking about and wanted her to know it.

She told how Russell bought a little New Testament to give to his adversary. He asked his mother what he should write in it. She wisely left that for him to decide.

She told the rapt listeners that he wrote three words in it. "Do you know what those three words were?" she asked. A couple of answers were ventured, but the memorable one came from the little boy who could identify with Russell's predicament.

Loud enough for the congregation to hear, he said, "LEAVE ME ALONE!" Appreciative laughter filled the auditorium.

Now that's the kind of thing many of us would have done. It's a natural response, but Russell wrote something a cut above natural.

In his own boyish handwriting, he wrote, "God Loves You." That, coupled with an invitation to come to Sunday School, turned an enemy into a friend.

Jesus said we have to become as little children to enter the Kingdom of Heaven. Without realizing it, a child was putting into practice what Jesus taught on a hillside long ago. "Blessed are the peacemakers: for they shall be called the children of God" (Matthew 5:9).

By love and God's Word, a balled-up fist can be turned into an outstretched hand. But these have to be

183

demonstrated and applied by someone who lives by God's rules.

There are raised fists the world over, inflicting untold suffering. It was that way in the days of Jesus and has been ever since the fall of man. Much of that anger and hate were directed at Him. Yet, never at His accusers did He shout, "LEAVE ME ALONE!"

On the contrary, He said, "Love your enemies, bless them that curse you, do good to them that hate you, and pray for them which despitefully use you, and persecute you" (Matthew 5:44). That's not the "natural" thing human nature tells us to do.

That's what Jesus said, that's what He did. He would say to us, "Go, and do thou likewise."

A hand of friendship is better than a fist. Every time.

SECTION 9

The Bible Used and Abused

185

Heart Transplant

"Out of the mouth of babes" often come words of wisdom. Like something Taylor Jones, not yet four, said.

He was asking Booma, his grandmother, about different characters or animals in stories he had heard read to him or seen on his video tapes. He wanted to know if they would hurt you. Being assured that the ones mentioned were harmless, he then asked about Peter Pan and Captain Hook.

Peter Pan passed the test, but what about Captain Hook? "Well," cautioned Booma, "he might hurt you." The little fella's serious reply was, "He needs to read the Bible!"

He hit the nail on the head. That is the only real solution to the problems of crime, violence, and the wanton disregard for human life, which are like a mega-mudslide about to bury the world.

Through listening to Bible stories, Taylor knows that reading the Bible is supposed to change the way a person behaves. Grownups know that Bible reading must be teamed up with believing in Jesus and obeying His word, but even a child knows the Bible can show bad people how to become good.

Laws are necessary, keeping us from anarchy. Education is imperative, enlightening the mind. Environment impacts conduct. These are important but cannot reach the root of the problem—the heart. Band-Aids do little good when radical surgery is needed.

The Bible declares the heart to be "desperately wicked," verified by those who get their thrills by hurting others. Then there are those whose hearts are fixed on doing good toward friends and strangers. The condition of the heart determines the difference.

Now God is the great heart surgeon. He says, "I will take the stony heart out of their flesh, and will give them a heart of flesh: that they may walk in My statutes, and keep My ordinances, and do them" (Ezekiel 11:19-20). Talk about a heart transplant and recovery! And He has one available for everyone who is willing to swap a mean heart for a good one. Just ask the person who has one.

There's a story of a man whose Model T Ford broke down. A benevolent stranger stopped and had the car running in no time. "How did you know what was wrong?" he was asked. "I made it," replied Henry Ford.

God knows how to fix us, because He made us. The instruction book is called the Bible.

Bible Clobbering

The Bible is bound to be a tough book. It's been misquoted, misinterpreted, misunderstood, and just plain missed. It's been denied, doubted, debated, declared full of errors, and doomed. It's been pounded on, prattled about, pushed aside, and put down.

Yet the Bible is as durable as God. It is in the hands of more people than ever, speaks through ever-growing numbers of translations, and like an anvil, outlasts all hammers. Isaiah said, "The word of our God shall stand forever" (Isaiah 40:8). Amazing how it withstands all abuse and keeps right on speaking authoritatively.

The Bible becomes a club for clobbering when used by some spiritually ignorant brother to prove his point. Doesn't matter if the interpretation is a country mile from the truth. You can whip a fellow in line that way or justify your own self for not doing what you should do. For instance.

A man refused ever to hear me preach again because I went to a movie theater. Now this was in the pre-X, R, PG days, so most of them wouldn't canker your morals. You'd come out about as clean as you went in—depending on what you took in.

Now to my condemner, even "Snow White" was bound to have been filmed in the caverns of Satan. And he had Scripture to prove it. The fact is, I had been to see a movie on the life of Martin Luther.

Folks just think the Bible doesn't say anything against going to picture shows. A "careful" study of Acts 19 will convince the uninformed. Paul's preaching had cut into the profit of the silversmiths who made little silver thingamajigs honoring the goddess Diana. Created an uproar and they gathered in the theater. Paul wanted to have a talk with them, but some friends "sent unto him, desiring him that he would not adventure himself into the theater" (Acts 19:31).

Plainly they said, "Don't go into the theater." There you have it. Everybody knows the words "theater" and "movies" are interchangeable!

Now the reason they warned him was to save him from getting his skull cracked. Right good advice. But my adversary had him a Bible verse to make it wrong for the preacher to look at a moving picture and right for *him* to stay home from church.

The Bible is not a dummy to be manipulated by a ventriloquist. It is the Word of God, free to say what it has to say. When rightly understood, the Word of Truth says, "Move over ignorance, I'm coming through!"

There are texts and contexts in Scripture. Better to let them dwell together in wedded bliss than to divorce them and make ourselves look foolish.

The Bible: A Mirror

Upon arising one morning, I looked into the mirror. The mirror said: "Your face could stand washing, and you've got bags under your eyes. Your hair looks as if you stuck your finger into a 220 electrical socket. You need to shave that white, scraggly beard. Where is your partial plate? Did you misplace your glasses? You have no shirt and tie on. You look like something only a wife or mother could love."

I didn't dare ask, "Mirror, mirror on the wall, who's the fairest of them all?" I knew the answer would be, "Not you, buddy."

Since all the mirror seemed to do was find fault, I took a stick and smashed it to smithereens.

Now anyone who believes the above tirade probably would believe the Brooklyn Bridge is for sale.

What really happened is that mirror revealed the truth. So I washed my face, combed my hair, shaved, put my plate in, my glasses on, donned a shirt and tie and hoped to be acceptable by more folks than immediate family members. I could say, "Mirror, mirror on the wall, You are my friend after all."

Now the Bible is like a mirror. When looked into honestly, it peels off the camouflage, making us aware of the truth about self. If disturbing, we can slam it shut in denial and return it to its dust-collecting shelf.

It can be like the person who hears God's words and refuses to act accordingly. The Bible says, "He looks into a mirror, then goes on his way, forgetting what he saw" (James 1:23-24, Paraphrased).

A remote-region missionary tells of an aged native woman who saw her reflection for the first time in his only mirror. At her insistence, he reluctantly agreed to sell it to her. She promptly broke it and triumphantly said, "There. You'll never tell on ME again!" Truth can be painful.

On the other hand, the same Bible that reveals our flaws holds before us the cleaned-up life we can have in Jesus. Consider looking into this looking glass: "If any man be in Christ, he is a new creation: old things are passed away; behold, all things are become new" (2 Corinthians 5:17). Man alive!

Jesus offers to do for us on the inside what looking respondingly into a wall mirror does on the outside. We get cleaned up and become presentable to God and man. Spiritually speaking, we get our "hair combed" and our "faces washed." Jesus doesn't apply "makeup"; He makes over.

Maybe we ought to say, "Bible, Bible, on the shelf, Come on down: show me myself." Could be quite a revelation—and spark a revolution.

God's Gandy Dancer

On "Twenty Years on the Road," Charles Kuralt told of the Gandy Dancers—a slang term for railroad workers or section hands. The "Gandy" was a long steel bar, like a giant crowbar, named for the Gandy Manufacturing Company. It was used to settle gravel around the crossties or to realign track. The "dancer" had something to do with the foot movement of the workers.

The dancers would insert their gandies under a section of crooked track and sing a little ditty. One went something like this: "What do you do, when the food runs out? Stand in the corner with your mouth shoved out." Then, altogether, they would pull on their bars. The track would straighten right up or a curve would move into proper radius, just like it's supposed to be.

Trains have to run on reliable tracks or they make tracks in the dirt. No doubt wrecks were avoided because the gandy dancers walked the tracks, doing their job.

One simple, profound spiritual truth emerges from Mr. Kuralt's fascinating story: The Bible is God's "Gandy Dancer."

The Bible will straighten up a person's life. And I do mean UP, for the natural bent of life is DOWN. It's been that way ever since Satan sold Adam and Eve a bill of goods in the Garden of Eden. Mankind's tracks have been about as straight as a corkscrew from then 'til now. He's made many a track in the dirt.

The myriad of laws on the books testify to man's inclination to jump the tracks. They help, but the problem is in the heart.

The Bible gets to the heart of the matter. "God saw that the wickedness of man was great in the earth, and that every imagination of the thoughts of his heart was only evil continually" (Genesis 6:5). That's crooked track, written about the human condition in Noah's day. Sounds for the world like today's headlines.

Enter the "Gandy Dancer." "Thy Word have I hid in mine heart, that I might not sin against Thee" (Psalm 119:11). Like a loving father encouraging his boy to live good, that's motivation to line up and do right.

The Bible, like the gandy dancer's steel bar, has to be applied where the kinky places are. It speaks to every temptation and sin known to man - pride, greed, lust, adultery and uncountable other wrongs as plentiful as crossties.

Thankfully, the Bible tells of Jesus Who offers to keep us on the straight and narrow way, for it grieves Him to see any life wrecked.

God's "Gandy Dancer" is able to make all the crooked places straight, being "profitable...for correction, for instruction in righteousness" (2 Timothy 3:16).

It also becomes life's railway to heaven.

Right Bible—Wrong Verse

A poor choice of words can create a situation as awkward as having two left feet. It's true even when the words are Scripture. "All Scripture is given by inspiration of God" (2 Timothy 3:16), but all portions of it are not appropriate for all occasions.

I know a preacher who went to visit his aged and infirmed aunt. The dear soul had had her leg amputated and needed all the comforting she could get. The nephew-preacher wore two hats: kinfolk and minister.

After a time of visiting and refreshments, a Scripture and prayer time seemed appropriate. So the nephew drew the "Sword of the Lord" from its shirt pocket sheath and made a selection. He must not have asked for guidance from the Lord. A portion of what he read fit about as well as a size five shoe on a size ten foot.

The passage was Psalm 121. A fine Scripture it is that has comforted and encouraged a host of folks. His ministerial tone conveyed the message real well until he hit verse three. "He will not suffer thy foot to be moved." That's what it says. Well, sir, there sat the beloved aunt in her wheelchair being ministered unto (?), and her foot had been re-moved!

Sometimes it's best to stay on your horse and keep riding. That's what he did, hoping no one caught on. Maybe the prayer he offered was a little more in keeping with the situation. Anyhow, the verse in question was about as appropriate as pronouncing the benediction at the beginning of a service.

That same Psalm assures us that "The Lord shall preserve thy going out and thy coming in" (Psalm 121:8). The preacher wished he could've gone out the back door and come in the front to give it another try.

I guess the Lord knows better than to expect perfection out of His imperfect servants. He just might appreciate it, though, if we'd use the common sense He gave us.

"For ever, O Lord, Thy word is settled in heaven" (Psalm 119:89). At times, the way handled on earth is a bit unsettling.

Revelry Vs. Reverence

Midnight of December 31, 1984 had a surprisingly beautiful old-year conclusion.

While watching the Hollywood-led revelers of New York do their thing on television, I noticed an absence of any thought that God might have something to do with an old year expiring and the birthday of a new year. To the Christian conscience, that made Him an absentee God, remote and ignored. He might as well have been relegated to the "black hole" of His universe.

Just as the lighted Big Apple was descending on the T.V. screen, counting off the final seconds of 1984, the clock-radio unexpectedly came on. A Christian station was going off the air. "To God Be the Glory" was being sung, followed by a prayer and climaxed with "The Hallelujah Chorus." The blaring T.V. was muted as

God's Presence filled the room. What a glorious way to end the old and begin the new!

"To God be the glory, great things He has done!" That's looking back, with notes of praise. The prayer: thanksgiving and petition. That's past and future. "King of kings and Lord of lords"—acknowledging Jesus, always. Hallelujah!

If we want a sure-fire, bang-up, undefeatable year, we should walk in the light of one of God's great promises: "In *all* thy ways acknowledge Him, and He shall direct thy paths" (Proverbs 3:6).

Draw a line through the middle of that verse. One side is ours; the other, God's. It is for us to acknowledge Him (worship, praise, talk with Him, trust), it is for Him to guide us. To cross over the line is to court disaster. To choose our own way into the unforeseen is like asking a blind man to guide us along a steep precipice.

When God shows us His path, it becomes our responsibility to walk on it—with Him. The following year can be the best, most exciting year ever, if we learn to submit ourselves to God in *all* directions and actions we are to face. His ways may not always be the most popular, but they are always right.

The Lord's path is always a good "foot path."

A Message from Mother

Mother and I were sitting at the kitchen table when I told her that her doctor had said she could no longer live alone.

She did not want to leave her home, having lived there for most of her seventy-six years. Yet, there was a look of relief in her eyes at the thought of having someone to care for her. The burden had become too heavy.

With the family history of Alzheimer's disease, I knew something of what the future would hold. I did not know that in the midst of many tears and much sorrow there would be moments of indescribable glory.

We placed her in the Baptist Retirement Home, knowing that excellent, loving care would be provided. At first, Mother thought she was back in her college dormitory and would declare from time to time that she had learned everything she needed to know and was ready to go home. Whenever I prepared to leave after a visit, she would say, "I'll go home with you."

For awhile we would receive letters written in her beautiful school teacher's hand. Then she forgot how to write and to read. She forgot her children and grandchildren and even the memory of her husband who had died four years before her illness. She had always said of him, "He was the best man in the world."

For several years after entering the retirement home, she played the piano for Sunday School and sang the old songs in her sweet soprano voice. When those gifts were taken from her memory, she still responded in some way to the sound of music.

One day I noticed that several pages had been torn from her Bible. I took it home with me for safekeeping. As I turned the pages, searching for passages of scripture which she had underlined, I came across a verse in the twenty-first chapter of the Book of John. As Jesus spoke to Peter, He said, "When you were younger, you girded yourself and walked where you wished; but when you are old, you will stretch out your hands, and another will gird you and carry you where you do not wish" (NKJV).

At first, I was puzzled. Why did Mother underline that verse? Then I knew, and my heart filled with sadness. I looked at the top of that same page, and there, written in a trembling hand, were the words, "Trust in Jesus." My heart was lifted by this message of faith which she had left for me.

Her longing for home remained, but her trust in Jesus would sustain her.

For fifteen long years the cruelty of Alzheimer's gradually took away the person she had been. In her last years she lay locked in a fetal position, unable to move or speak.

I had prayed that, when the time came, she would not die alone. God answered my prayers. We were able to be at her side for two days and two nights before the end came. On the last night of her earthly life, my sister and I and our husbands sat by her bedside, singing the songs she loved so well. The kind nurses assured us our singing was welcomed, and we would disturb no one.

At midnight, quietly and peacefully, she drew her last breath. I said to my sister, "Look at her face." At the age of ninety-one, her skin was smooth and clear, but now, there was a glow—a luminous, pearl-like glow—a look of glory!

We stood there in awe of this beauty, and in those moments we knew she was seeing the One whom she had trusted all those long years. At last, she was truly home.

—By Harriett Jones

SECTION 10

God Will Take Care of You

From Sinking Sand

Competitive trail-riding must be thrilling for those so inclined to indulge. To stay on the trail means the rider can sing "Happy Trails to You." To get off the trail changes the tune.

The ride was near Clemson, SC. Our son, Mark, a national champion among the American Trail Riders, was there for a sixty mile competitive event. The Trail Master marks the trail ahead of time with ribbons and maps to follow.

The riders were warned about the dangers of the sandy creek bottoms and were urged to stay on the trail. Only trouble, though, Mark arrived too late to attend the briefing. He missed the wise counsel of the one who knew the way.

After riding for several miles, enjoying the beautiful scenery, he decided it was time to water his horse. A nearby creek looked inviting.

The uninformed horseman left the trail at a place where "stay on the trail" was clearly marked. The horse began to drink, when, without warning, he sank to his chest and to Mark's knees in quicksand. With an instinct for survival uppermost in his mind, he immediately rolled over the horse's head and landed upside down in the creek. He could say with the Psalmist, "Save me, O God! For the waters have come up to my neck. I sink in deep mire, where there is no standing" (Psalm 69:1-2, NKJV).

Dripping wet, he stood by helplessly as his horse struggled to get free. Since trail horses are bred for endurance, Mark's horse succeeded—only to sink twice more before getting on solid ground.

To hear this story from our son gave these parents a sinking feeling. What could have been a tragedy had a happy ending.

Life is much like a trail-ride. There are dangers along the way as well as much beauty. Thankfully, Jesus, like the Trail Master, has gone before us to mark the way. Better still, He said, "I *am* the way" (John 14:6). He gives us an invitation to follow Him. He knows where the sandy bogs are and will steer us away from them—if we let Him.

Problems develop when a person misses the "briefing." God's briefing for a safe journey is found in the Bible. When the uninstructed strike out on their own and get off the trail, they become bogged down in the sinking sands of life. Jesus is there to deliver us. And from those sinking sands, He lifts us to safety on solid ground.

Following the instructions of the Trail Master is important. Trail-riding involves a great deal of struggle for the horse and rider. However, there is a deep sense of satisfaction when both come safely into camp. There are rewards for a ride well done.

Likewise, the living of our lives on this earth involves many struggles. When we keep our eyes on the trail Jesus has marked for us and do not turn aside to our own path, there is a deep sense of satisfaction in knowing we have followed the way of our Master. He will one day reward us with the words, "Well done, thou good and faithful servant...enter thou into the joy of thy Lord" (Matthew 25:21).

Have a good and joyful ride.

Demands and Identification

If I knew to whom credit is due for this yarn, it would be given gladly. I heard it at a Baptist gathering. This version is somewhat embellished.

A college boy needed one more course for graduation. An old professor was famous for his crip course on birds. Maybe it was "Birdology" or a "fowl" course. The aspiring graduate enrolled. Easy, easy.

A dark cloud formed and descended on Wingtown. The old prof flew away to that great classroom in the sky.

Enter a new, young professor who believed in the work ethic for students. He was tough as a bird's beak, making them dig like a robin grubbing for worms.

Exam time. The test was a booklet with pictures of one hundred birds to be identified. What the teacher had done made the student's feather's fall and caused anger to flap his wings. With magic marker, all of the birds' bodies had been blacked out, leaving only their legs showing.

Hope for graduation diminished, as the flying bodiless bird book hit the wall. "Nobody could pass a test like that!" squawked the flappable student. He was as frustrated as an old crow with a broken cawer.

With ruffled feathers, the bird-brained instructor said, "Young man, what's your name?" Ah, sweet revenge was perched and ready for flight. The unidentified lad pulled his pant legs up, exposing his legs. "You tell me," he chirped.

A couple of thoughts are soaring around somewhere in this ridiculous story. They have to do with outlandish demands and identification—problems that folks frequently face. Real sticklers at times. Some "bird" demands more than we can give or considers us little more than a number— a faceless cog in the machinery of life.

Not so with God. He is the compassionate Teacher who makes the course of life demanding but not impossible. Exam time is not some unanswerable question to trip us up but an examination of the heart to know that "Christ, the hope of glory" abides there.

Our identification is "written in the Lamb's book of life" (Revelation 21:27) and cannot be erased. "The Lord knoweth them that are His" (2 Timothy 2:19).

Jesus doesn't have to ask, "Young man, what's your name?" If we were to ask Him if He knows who we are, He would tell us, "We met at Calvary; I have never forgotten you."

Perhaps we can catch a glimpse of grandeur beyond the bird leg story. If so, we begin to feel a stirring in our hearts to fly to the bosom of the Heavenly Father. And then we sing, "I'll fly away, oh glory, I'll fly away" to the Christian's eternal nesting place.

Tithing and Tires

As the Israelites gathered just enough manna for each day's need, so God often supplies just enough for some particular need today.

The tires on my car had about worn themselves out with all of that ministerial ministering. It was time to re-tire. That called for money.

Son Mark had sent his pop two hundred bucks for Father's Day for new tires. Twenty of that belonged to the Lord, since tithing is what He recommends. (Actually He says bring it.) There's a built-in blessing promised. That left a hundred and eighty. I was about to see how the God who promises to supply all our needs would.

Now for a preacher to ask for a discount, because he is a preacher, discounts the ministry. Makes business folks dread to see him come to do business. It's more in keeping with his profession to trust the Lord to take care of his needs in His own way. Sometimes He comes up with a dandy.

I hauled myself down to Nu-Tread, my favorite tire-buying place. Friend Mike Ray advised me what kind to buy. Later, when I went to pick up my newly-shod chariot, looking at the bill made my eyes sorta bulge.

Voluntarily, without any pitiful look on my part, Mike had figured the tires at his cost, balanced and mounted them, (even washed them) and aligned the front end. Total cost - $180.72! I was seventy-two cents in the hole. All of that for seventy-two cents. But hold on; there's more.

After I told the incident at a preacher's breakfast, and praised the Lord for His goodness, one big-hearted reverend pulled out a dollar and gave it to me! Glory; would the Lord never cease! A dime of that was the Lord's, leaving me eighteen cents to the good. Out of sheer gratitude, it seemed reasonable to give God the whole dollar.

At the end of the forty year trek in the wilderness, the Lord said to the Israelites, "Thy shoe is not waxen old upon thy foot" (Deuteronomy 29:5). Now I don't expect those tires from the Lord to last forty years; forty thousand miles will do nicely. I'll tell you what I do expect: when they have gone the last mile of the way, another set will be provided.

A person can learn heavenly truths through earthly things. When Jesus taught us to pray, "Give us this day our daily bread," it must have meant tires, too.

Grace Like the Sea

The mighty Atlantic lapped the sandy beach. The Creator's POWER was evident in the emerald-green waves, wearing their white caps. The sustained roar of the sea sounded like an old agitated lion. The overcast sky hovered like a gray spotted canopy, blotting out the blue.

The landing of a weather-whipped walkway served as a Chapel of the Heart. God's PRESENCE was there, making it a place of soul-searching for the wayfarer resting there. His emotions rose and fell like the tumbling tide.

His heart rose in praise, as he thought of the loving hand that had reached from heaven above. A hand filled with abounding blessings that covered a lifetime.

Low moments came when thoughts of past failures slipped through memory's door. They come to all. The Lord wants His forgiven children to have inner calm. But, like pirates, these intruders have a way of creating havoc.

Those "I wish they'd go away" memories clamor for attention, often nearly drowning the rememberer in self-condemnation. Sometimes wringing tears from the eyes.

The sea, vast in width, vast in depth, encouraged a lingering gaze. Gradually, an oft-forgotten truth about the grace of God awakened. Sin is a tragic part of life, but the repentant heart makes a discovery. God promises that He "will cast all of our sin into the depths of the sea" (Micah 7:19).

Now grace, like the sea, is a place of depth where things confessed are to be left, never to be seen again. And, like the sunken Titanic, all thoughts of an attempted raising of past regrets should be resisted, looked upon as useless and unprofitable.

Symbolically, the sea is a burying place for our sins. In reality, "The blood of Jesus cleanses from all unrighteousness" (1 John 1:7). That means they are covered.

In the heart of the "Beach-Pilgrim," he knew that God's grace is indeed greater than all his sin. His spirit began to rise like the flight of the seagulls with the wind beneath their wings. He knew, too, there would be future times when human frailty will have other debris to cast into the absorbing depths of the Father's grace. He hopes he will then remember the sea.

As Jesus calmed the troubled waters of the Sea of Galilee, so He brings peace to the troubled heart. Especially the heart that tastes the immeasurable dimension of God's amazing, incomprehensible grace.

> God's grace, like the ocean
> Has its unfathomed deeps:
> The surface is revealed,
> Unseen myst'ry it keeps.

Within that mystery is God's promise to the repentant: "I will be merciful to their unrighteousness, and their sins and their iniquities will I remember no more" (Hebrews 8:12).

An old deacon once prayed in a picturesque way, "O Lord, forgive our sins, and throw 'em in the sea of forgetness."

That's where they are. It's best to leave 'em there.

Heavenly Vision

Stuart Henderson and I flew to Shatley Springs in the mountains for a delicious family-style lunch. His trusty little Citabria plane became an observatory for some lofty thoughts.

The absolute importance of the propeller rose to the surface of my mind. Whirling faster than eye can see confirmed it was there, carrying the plane on the sky's highway. Without it, we would have remained grounded.

Mankind is pretty much earthbound but with a built-in longing for higher things. It's the way our Creator intended.

Archie Campbell, of "Hee-Haw" fame, said he was a white-knuckle flyer. Meaning he was scared to fly. Looking through the window, he said to his seatmate, "Look down there; people look like ants." His fellow-traveler replied: "They ARE ants; we haven't taken off yet."

As the propeller lifts the wings of the plane, so God lifts us and causes us to fly on the "wings of the wind" (Psalm 18:10).

Things look altogether different when you see them from up, looking down. There were tilled fields, winding ribbon-like roads, placid lakes and meandering rivers, variably-colored trees, hump-backed mountains, cities, and churches. The panoramic world looked like a beautiful unfolding tapestry.

So the things of this earth appear to be less troubling and more beautiful when seen from a heavenly viewpoint. For God has given us new eyes with which to see.

Flying is not always smooth. The air got a little rough on the way home. Felt like some road builder needed to get up there with his grader to smooth out the ruts. But, thanks to the faithful propeller, we hit the bumps without falling.

God does not promise there will be no broken places on our earthly journey. Even though we are jostled about at times, we can say with the Psalmist, "In the shadow of Your wings I will take my refuge, until these calamities have passed by" (Psalm 57:1, NKJV).

A Rainbow and a Cross

God has many ways of showing His hand. Life is made up of storms and calms. Storms can blow our dreams and hopes to smithereens. With unanswered "whys" amidst the debris, our heavenly Father often gives visible assurance that quietens the aching heart.

Polly Wilson courageously did battle with a deadly foe, cancer. For six years it would advance and retreat, finally winning. As always, its victory left a trail of sorrow. Sorrow that never fully goes away.

An appropriately fitting service was conducted at the graveside in Bear Swamp Baptist Church's cemetery. There, the body of this lovely Christian lady was numbered among the many others who had preceded her through the shadowy valley.

Gathered family and friends left the bit of now-hallowed ground, carrying grief of varying weights. Grief, awash with tears.

Late in the afternoon, the sky donned a black robe. Lightning scribbled threatening messages on the clouds, as ol' thunder clapped his hands. Rain, like great tears, pounded the earth. It was almost as if nature was empathizing with the storms raging in heaving breasts of the left-lonely family.

Supportive friends had provided lunch at the church. The evening meal would be leftovers from the abundant noon meal, plus fresh additions.

As we gathered at the meeting house, the roughhouse storm had moved on. Only gentle tears dropped from the sky. Polly's brother-in-law, Samuel Ray, said, "Come here. Look!"

God had set a rainbow in the sky. There's nothing unusual about that, for He has been doing it ever since Noah's day. It had to do with a promise He made. And to look beyond the rainbow would be to think of God.

Now what gave this bow in the sky special meaning was this: the end of it was pointing directly above the tent erected over Polly's resting place. Some say there's a pot of gold at the end of the rainbow. That's penny stuff compared to what we saw that day. God was manifesting His Presence, keeping His promise of receiving His own unto Himself. It was as though Polly's spirit had caught a ride on the rainbow, only to find herself in heaven.

One other touch of glory. A light streak of cloud was seen cutting across the rainbow, making the shape of a cross. What a combination! A rainbow promising life over death and a cross to remind of God's great gift of salvation through Jesus.

God's hand wrote a message in the sky that day. A message of hope, comfort, love, victory. He said it a long time ago: "Death is swallowed up in victory" (I Corinthians 15:54).

When the message is believed, the tempest in the heart begins to subside. And the emptiness is filled with the Presence of God.

A crossbow in the hands of an enemy means death. A Bow-Cross from God is life.

No, Never Alone

Nobody likes to be bored with operation stories. Like the time a foot operation required a cast up to my knee. As I hobbled about at a Baptist Convention, one sympathetic preacher said, "I don't want to know what happened; I just want you to know I'm sorry."

There I stood, all primed and ready to go into detail about what had happened, and he didn't want to hear it. Was I evermore disappointed! His "I'm sorry" was sufficient and long remembered. We both were spared the sob story.

Watch out now; here comes one. If you wade through the recounting of it, an application to life will be found. So, read on.

Triple-bypass heart surgery is not in the fun category. One consents to it out of sheer necessity, because of the desire to live on a while longer.

They load you up on "don't care" pills and shots, put you on a gurney, and wheel you into the dissecting room. I was told later what they had done to me. (Glad I didn't know beforehand.)

After you are strapped down, your chest is sawed open (chainsaw?), pried apart, a vein is removed from a leg. Heart arteries and leg vein are united in wedlock, to live happily everafter. Then you are stapled up, cleaned up and, in complete oblivion, carted to intensive care. A day or so slips by, but you are somewhere in outer space. Thankfully.

When judged appropriate, you take up residence in a prepared private room. Not knowing anything, you could not care less. At least you feel no pain. Yet.

(By now, dear reader, tears should be flowing down your face.)

Between early Thursday morning and five o'clock Saturday morning, I knew about as much as a surgeon who had never studied medicine. Then the real world poked his head in the door, bringing me back from my nether world.

I had about as much knowledge of where I was and what had happened as a newborn baby. Thought I was in some basement somewhere. Foggy, foggy.

But do you know what? To my right there sat the finest sight I had seen in nearly forty-eight hours: our son, Mark. His face was like the face of an angel. His word, "Daddy," was as comforting and refreshing as a flowing mountain stream. And I knew that I had not been alone.

All through my hospital stay, I was never alone. Day and night, either my wife or one of our four children or some caring friend was there. Anytime I awakened, I could see a loving face and a hand of help reaching out. Friend, that will carry you through piled-up troubles.

Calamities overtake us all. We may get hurt but not destroyed. There's nothing that we and the Lord together can't handle. He is there all the time. Just like the Bible says, "They shall call His name Emmanuel, which being interpreted is, God with us." What a promise!

Reaching In: Reaching Up

A chill was in the blustery wind, the sky dull and cloudy, and the whitecapped ocean waves overlapped each other to have a moment on the waiting beach.

A gray-haired man with a slight limp slowly made tracks in the sand, knowing he had walked farther in life than he would walk again. His unseen friend accompanied him. They had spent a lifetime together, each knowing all about the other. For they are body and soul. No one else was in sight.

The weatherbeaten beachhouse steps offered a place of rest. A good place to think, to remember. His melancholy mood matched the weather. The past, with its failings, began crowding his mind.

There were memories of lost opportunities for good that had knocked, and, when unanswered, moved on. Recollections of things done that should never have been done and things not done that should have been. Words better not said and words not said that needed to be said.

The bowed head indicated a deep inner searching. He knew the meaning of heartache and thought of hearts he had caused to ache. He thought of youthful ambitions and dreams that never became anything but dreams.

There was the awareness of God's multiple blessings and gratitude for whatever good was accomplished. But, at the moment, he was more aware of what his life might have been. The ocean mist on his bifocals and tears made it hard to see anything. Anything but God.

The heart intuitively knows there has to be more to life than we know now and that there is a place of fulfillment where failure is not known. A longing flooded the chamber of his soul. From its depths a cry came forth that seemed to blend with the ocean's rhythm: "O God, Thou who hast created the mighty ocean and every grain of sand, have mercy on me!"

Presently, a cleansing calm began to settle within, the wind helped dry his eyes, and he moved on. On, toward whatever steps remain to be taken. On, in the knowledge that there is no perfection in this life and that God's mercy covers his imperfections. On, assured that he can walk the rest of the way usefully—and with joy.

Then, he remembered God's promise of a new heaven and earth, and the sweet refrain echoed in his heart: "God shall wipe away all tears from their eyes; and there shall be no more death, neither sorrow, nor crying, neither shall there be any more pain...Behold I make all things new!" (Revelation 21:4-5)

And the gray-haired man knew that the indescribable something within that reaches for perfection will be satisfied. For heaven is such a place. A place of redemption for the redeemed. Failure and regret will have vanished like the fog over the ocean when the sun breaks through the clouds.

With his hand in the great Savior's hand, he walks with renewed strength toward the setting of the sun. And its rising!

Homeplace

The word "Homeplace" conjures up memories. Good ones, if good things happened there. Like one such place in Halifax County, my wife's family homeplace.

Her "Papa" (grandfather) cut the trees, planed the lumber, and built the house. Floors weren't always level, corners not exactly square. Some areas would shake and creak in response to footsteps.

Papa farmed his fifty acres, carried the mail on horseback, and served as a Magistrate. There was always enough for the needs of the family and much to share with friends. School teachers boarded there, the circuit-riding preacher found a place to lay his head, and even strangers were welcomed to stay.

This rambling house was home for the fifteen children born into Mammy and Papa's family. Though not built by a skilled craftsman, it had durability. It was a gathering place for family members, relatives, and friends.

A big black wood stove stood in the kitchen. Hot biscuits and country ham were among the favorite foods Mammy and her children cooked. Blue willow dishes graced the table. A coffee grinder that hung on the wall ground out many a cup of Luzianne coffee with chicory.

Good food, laughter, instrumental music, and harmonizing made it a special place. Best of all, love and a reverence for God gave it strength and character. Jesus was the unseen but very real Guest, giving life meaning. Papa learned the hymns with the help of a tuning fork and led the singing at nearby Bear Swamp Baptist Church.

Mammy outlived Papa by a good number of years. On holidays and weekends, all roads seemed to lead to "Mammy's house." There were times when sorrow would pay a visit. Four of the children did not survive their early years. But the joys far outweighed the sorrows. The walls were storage places for the good memories that were created there: memories that forked out in every direction wherever members of the family and acquaintances went.

Three generations lived in the homeplace. There came a time when the last member of the family living there could no longer manage alone. The property was sold and became home for someone else. Though the house had been modernized, the piled-up years had taken their toll. The end of a long era was in sight.

Some of the doors, heart-pine lumber and the nearly fifteen-inch-wide baseboards were removed. The rest of the house was no match for the bulldozer's shamble-making power. That which had stood for eighty-five years was hauled down into the woods to become a part of the earth from which it had originated.

We can't go home anymore—except by taking a sentimental journey in mind and heart. As long as anyone lives, whose life was touched by that hallowed spot, the "homefires" will keep burning. The sound of music will waft hauntingly in the deep recesses of the mind, laughter will echo in the heart, and love will fill the soul. Most likely a slow, plaintive smile will grace the face of the rememberer.

Life is something like the homeplace. We originate, grow, and learn the meaning of the joys and sorrows that touch us. But we grow old. Finally the time comes when the "old house" can't be fixed anymore. We move out, the house returns to dust, and we become a memory to those who knew and loved us. But the eternal life of the Christian goes beyond all of that.

Through Jesus, we can say: "For we know that if the earthly tent we live in is destroyed, we have a building from God, a house not made with hands, eternal in the heavens" (2 Corinthians 5:1, NRSV).

The song writer said, "Change and decay in all around I see, O Thou Who changest not, abide with me" (from the hymn, "Abide with Me"). And He does.

That which is temporal becomes eternal. Our homeplace then is with our Heavenly Father, world without end. Amen.

—By Crate and Harriett Jones

Epilogue

There are friends seen and friends unseen. Because you have read this book, we have become a part of each other. As I have shared my heart with you, it is my prayer that you have been drawn closer to our Savior, Jesus Christ. I want Him to be real to you. This desire can be illustrated in this closing story.

My aunts, Ibo and Ida B., had lived together all of their lives. They worked at the same candy factory and finally occupied the same room in a nursing home. They never married and were inseparable.

There came the time when Ibo could say with Paul, "The time of my departure is at hand." She was translated into heaven at the age of one-hundred-and-one.

Not long before she died, she said this: "I don't guess I'll ever get to go to church anymore. I always loved to go to church, and I loved to sing the hymns. My two favorite hymns are 'Will There Be Any Stars in My Crown' and 'It Is Well with My Soul.' " Then, thoughtfully, she added, "And it IS well with my soul."

Her ninety-one-year-old surviving sister, Ida B., whose thinking was not always clear, kept going about the nursing home, looking for her sister. It would slip her mind that Ibo had died. She would say, "Where's Ibo?" Dit, my sister, and their Angel of Mercy, said to her, "Ibo is in heaven with Mamaw. Someday, we'll go to be with them." Ida B. thought for a moment and replied, "And they will say, 'Here they come!' "

If this book has helped you on your journey in life and to heaven, all praise to the Lord!

Your friend,
Crate Jones

"For God so loved the world, that He gave His only begotten Son, that whosoever believeth in Him should not perish, but have everlasting life"
(John 3:16).

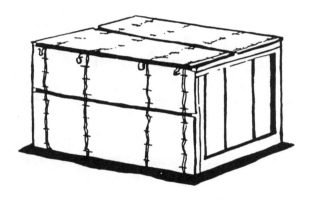

Additional copies may be ordered from:

Crate Jones
3106 Appling Way
Durham, NC 27703

Include $10.95 for each book plus shipping and handling as follows: $3 for first book and $1 additional for each additional book ordered.